THE MAKING OF

MISS POTTER

Garth Pearce

Photographs by
Alex Bailey

FREDERICK WARNE

DAVID KIRSCHNER PRODUCTIONS and PHOENIX PICTURES PRESENT IN
ASSOCIATION WITH ISLE OF MAN FILM IN ASSOCIATION WITH THE UK FILM
COUNCIL A CHRIS NOONAN FILM RENÉE ZELLWEGER EWAN McGREGOR
MISS POTTER
BILL PATERSON BARBARA FLYNN LLOYD OWEN and EMILY WATSON
Casting by PRISCILLA JOHN CDG Costume Designer ANTHONY POWELL
Music by NIGEL WESTLAKE Editor ROBIN SALES Production Designer MARTIN CHILDS
Director of Photography ANDREW DUNN BSC Executive Producers RENÉE ZELLWEGER
LOUIS PHILLIPS NIGEL WOOLL Produced by MIKE MEDAVOY DAVID KIRSCHNER
COREY SIENEGA ARNOLD W. MESSER DAVID THWAITES
Written by RICHARD MALTBY JR. Directed by CHRIS NOONAN

Acknowledgments

The publishers would like to thank the director, the producers, cast and crew for their kind cooperation
during the preparation of this book. Particular thanks are due to David Thwaites, Nigel Wooll and Susan
d'Arcy for their help in supplying information and material.

FREDERICK WARNE

Published by Penguin Group
Penguin Group (USA) Inc., 345 Hudson Street, New York, New York 10014, U.S.A.
Penguin Group (Canada), 90 Eglinton Avenue East, Suite 700, Toronto, Ontario, Canada M4P 2Y3
(a division of Pearson Penguin Canada Inc.)
Penguin Books Ltd, 80 Strand, London WC2R 0RL, England
Penguin Ireland, 25 St Stephen's Green, Dublin 2, Ireland (a division of Penguin Books Ltd)
Penguin Group (Australia), 250 Camberwell Road, Camberwell, Victoria 3124, Australia
(a division of Pearson Australia Group Pty Ltd)
Penguin Books India Pvt Ltd, 11 Community Centre, Panchsheel Park, New Delhi – 110 017, India
Penguin Group (NZ), Cnr Airborne and Rosedale Roads, Albany, Auckland 1310, New Zealand
(a division of Pearson New Zealand Ltd)
Penguin Books (South Africa) (Pty) Ltd, 24 Sturdee Avenue, Rosebank, Johannesburg 2196, South Africa

Penguin Books Ltd, Registered Offices: 80 Strand, London WC2R 0RL, England

Web site at: www.peterrabbit.com

First published by Frederick Warne in 2006

1 3 5 7 9 10 8 6 4 2

ISBN-13: 978-0-7232-5863-6
ISBN-10: 0-7232-5863-5
Design by Perfect Bound Ltd

Printed in U.S.A.

CONTENTS

Chapter One

FROM HOLLYWOOD TO THE ISLE OF MAN

'My first instinct when I was asked to do this was, "Do I really want to put myself through it?"'

Renée Zellweger slips out of her hotel room at dawn, her slight, slim figure dressed in a grey tracksuit. She crosses the wide sweep of the seafront road in Douglas, Isle of Man. The only other person on view is a virtual dot in the distance, walking a dog along the promenade. She then begins her first task of the day, pounding the pavements for half an hour, overlooked by rows of Victorian seaside houses, all blind to her efforts, with curtains still drawn.

Zellweger, 37, toils alone and in silence. Her hair is tucked under a peaked cap, and she keeps her head down while striding fiercely into the wind. It is as if she had added a pair of blinkers to her head-gear. She follows an intensely-focused process to create her new character, to the exclusion of all else.

Zellweger's approach has already won remarkable results in a career which went into overdrive when she was chosen by Tom Cruise to play his Girl Friday, Dorothy Boyd, in the 1996 film, *Jerry Maguire*. It has since won her an Oscar as best supporting actress for *Cold Mountain* (2003) and further Oscar nominations as best actress for the musical *Chicago* (2002) and *Bridget Jones's Diary* (2001).

She now faces what is arguably her toughest task: playing Beatrix Potter, who remains one of the world's most famous children's writers, more than a hundred years after the publication of her debut bestseller, *The Tale of Peter Rabbit*.

For an American actress who has already courted controversy by twice playing the fictional Bridget Jones, this is a dangerous step. She is not only playing an

English character once more, but an English icon. Bridget existed only in the mind of novelist Helen Fielding and her devoted readers. But Beatrix, who died on December 22nd, 1943, at the age of 77, lived a life which has been tracked and recorded by an army of fans and historians.

'I am more than aware of the question marks,' admits Zellweger. 'I am playing a character who is part of British history. Most people have heard of her, have read her books as a child or bought them for their own children. They all have an opinion. My first instinct when I was asked to do this was, "Do I really want to put myself through it?" Then I kept on returning to the script and starting to think of her story and what we could do with it. I became hooked. After that, it was a matter of doing what it takes.'

What privately appealed to Zellweger – who seems to do what it takes as a matter of course – was the similarity between Potter's approach to work and her own. They are both highly successful, enterprising artists, separated by a century of change. But the mood and opportunities for women in the early 1900s were very different. Potter, who lived a well-heeled life at home with her wealthy parents in South Kensington, London, worked to develop her independence in a world not really ready for women of success and means.

ABOVE *Preparations for the scene in an art gallery, with a prop table laden with the requirements*

OPPOSITE TOP
Renée Zellweger as Beatrix Potter

OPPOSITE BOTTOM
Director Chris Noonan

Zellweger, on the other hand, was university-educated in Texas – in the heart of the south in the United States, regarded as an exciting new world for many at the start of the last century – and was allowed the freedom to develop. She moved to Hollywood prepared to take her chances in film. Shortly before Cruise auditioned her for *Jerry Maguire*, she was serving drinks in a bar. After that, she progressed to become one of the world's most highly rated actresses.

The long process of bringing *Miss Potter* to the screen had begun in 1992 when the film's writer, 67-year-old Richard Maltby, Jr (see page 47), had first offered up his original Potter screenplay on spec. The script attracted interest from a number of producers, but it wasn't until David Kirschner and Corey Sienega took on the project with genuine commitment that things really started coming together. Their work on the screenplay ensured it had the right 'dramatic slant' for film. However, there was still a convoluted process ahead before the movie could begin in earnest.

It took a meeting at the 2003 Sundance Film Festival between Maltby's agent and young British producer David Thwaites, who works with former studio chief Mike Medavoy at Phoenix Pictures in Los Angeles, to get the ball rolling. Soon afterwards there was what David Kirschner describes as a 'joining together of forces' when he met with Thwaites and Medavoy to discuss the project. The deal, which was put together by another key producer, Arnie Messer, involved financing from Summit Entertainment, the UK Film Council's Premiere Fund, Grosvenor Park and the Isle of Man Film Commission. In Britain, the distribution rights had been snapped up by Momentum Pictures for UK and Spain even before the financing was finalized. The American distribution rights were bought by the Weinstein Company.

At last the film was set to go. The director, Chris Noonan (see page 55) was in place, prepared to direct his first film since 1995, when his story of a runaway pig, *Babe*, became an unexpected hit. Key figures in production and costumes were hired, as well as some big guns behind the cameras. The production designer was Martin Childs (see page 74) who had won an Oscar for his work on *Shakespeare in Love* (1998) and had somehow created a marvel out of a tiny budget for the 1997 film *Mrs Brown*. There was also veteran costume designer Anthony Powell (see page 69), who had enjoyed three Oscar successes for *Travels with my Aunt* (1972), *Death on the Nile* (1978) and *Tess* (1979). 'If the sun was shining, you'd get a suntan from the reflection of all the awards around here,' remarked one member of the film crew.

From Hollywood to the Isle of Man

There were also some classy additions to the cast. First, and probably most important, was the choice of Scottish actor Ewan McGregor (see page 35) to play Norman Warne, Beatrix's publisher and later fiancé. Emily Watson (see page 79), a former member of the Royal Shakespeare Company who won best actress Oscar nominations for *Breaking the Waves* (1996) and *Hilary and Jackie* (1998), was hired as Millie Warne, Norman's sister. Bill Paterson (see page 82), a consistently fine performer on television and in films like *The Killing Fields* and *Chaplin*, had agreed to play Beatrix's father, Rupert Potter. The equally reliable Barbara Flynn (see page 85), who played Mary Queen

of Scots opposite Helen Mirren's Queen Elizabeth in the recent television film, *Elizabeth 1*, was lined up to play Beatrix's snobbish mother, Helen Potter.

The filming began on Tuesday, March 7th, 2006 on the edge of west London, in a pretty little street called The Butts, Brentford. It started with high drama in front of the camera, since it featured the scene in which Beatrix arrives at the Warne household following the news of her fiancé's death.

The British-based film crew were soon to learn, though, that Zellweger's presence brings an added intensity to the set. She carefully works out what she can achieve in front of the camera for a few frantic weeks of filming. She then begins a painstaking process to create her character. Her early morning run is only a tiny part of the routine.

She follows a succession of targets. She involves herself in the design of her costumes, undergoes dialect coaching on a daily basis and rejects some of her own scenes the moment she's filmed them, as just not being good enough. She's her own ruthless critic and, it seems, she is never quite satisfied with anything she achieves. The real world is freeze-framed.

Her world becomes a script and a character, where every nuance and inflection of voice is learned by heart. She has researched Potter's history thoroughly, and become a member of the Beatrix Potter Society. She has also bought membership for the other main actors, as a gift. She's determined to get things right. Curiously, though, she does all this alone. There is no entourage, as there is so often with big-name performers.

OPPOSITE
Norman Warne (Ewan McGregor) arrives at the Reform Club to meet Beatrix's father

ABOVE *Director Chris Noonan with writer Richard Maltby, Jr*

BELOW *Artiste chairs on set. The front four are producers*

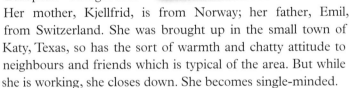

ABOVE *Costume designer Anthony Powell*

RIGHT *The independent-minded Millie (Emily Watson)*

BELOW *The perfect hosts – Bill Paterson and Barbara Flynn as Mr and Mrs Potter*

OPPOSITE *Beatrix (Renée Zellweger) tries to absorb the news of Norman's death*

Zellweger prefers to travel light and work heavy. Her only companion, her personal assistant Sarah, returned to America at one point during filming on the Isle of Man. It hardly sounds a big deal to those who work alone all the time, whether self-employed or at a desk. But in the ego-driven world of movies, where insecurities are constantly massaged by a team of hangers-on, it is unusual. Zellweger, though, is an unusual woman.

She comes from a European background. Her mother, Kjellfrid, is from Norway; her father, Emil, from Switzerland. She was brought up in the small town of Katy, Texas, so has the sort of warmth and chatty attitude to neighbours and friends which is typical of the area. But while she is working, she closes down. She becomes single-minded.

'She is not being unfriendly,' reports her dialect coach, Barbara Berkery (see page 31), who also prepared her for Bridget Jones. 'She is a perfectionist. It is that focus which sets her apart from the rest. To the normal eye or ear, everything she does sounds and looks good. But, to her, she wants something special. She knows when it is right. So she takes that extra step to try and make it perfect.'

Zellweger certainly tries for perfection at every moment. She does not turn a hair at being on the Isle of Man, the giant rock of an island set in the harsh Irish Sea, midway between the north-west English coast and Ireland. The location is a strange

The Making of Miss Potter

ABOVE *Filming in
the Lake District*

BELOW *The Potter
drawing room – built in a
shed on the Isle of Man*

one, in the sense that no scene in the film is supposed to be set on the island itself. Nor, indeed, are the island's fine craggy coastline or beautiful sweeping hills used as a backdrop. The principal exterior location scenes will be filmed later in the English Lake District. Instead, here in the Isle of Man the interiors of the Potters' large London house at 2, Bolton Gardens are sandwiched into a succession of farm buildings and an industrial estate. The reason is finance: the Isle of Man Film Commission, which has helped a total of seventy-eight different productions in the past, is providing twenty-five per cent of the *Miss Potter* $25 million budget.

The deal, as with other films, is that the producers make sure that at least half the film is made on the island, using its wide range of film services. So everything from car hire firms to hotels benefit from money spent. It works for the stars, too. The islanders are, by nature, low key and are used to seeing major Hollywood names and faces, of all ages, from Johnny Depp to Dame Julie Andrews, in their midst.

So, first in locations round London, then in the Isle of Man and finally in the Lake District, Beatrix Potter's life is being recreated and everyone works hard to make sure the settings look right and accuracy is respected.

Of course, to those who know the real story, there will be a few jarring notes. In reality, for example, Beatrix was in North Wales, not in the Lake District, when she heard of Norman's death but for both practical and artistic reasons it made sense to film the scene in the Lakes. There is also no evidence that she knew her first – and only – husband, solicitor William Heelis (Lloyd Owen) in childhood. But, for the most part, Potter devotees will embrace both the sense of atmosphere and authenticity in the film version of her life.

As for Renée Zellweger, she has worked assiduously towards the goal of making Miss Potter come alive. Her devotion to the role looks set to win wide support for both Beatrix and herself.

ABOVE *Warning sign from* Hopping Mad, *the production company formed for* Miss Potter

BELOW *Renée Zellweger in the Lake District*

Chapter Two

TAKE FIVE ~ IN THE BACK OF THE COWSHED

'There was a plane overhead – it sounds like the Battle of Britain.'

Renée Zellweger is picked up from her hotel by 7.30 every morning to go and work in a cowshed. The building, along a myriad of lanes on Lheakrow Farm on the edge of the small village of Foxdale, has been converted into a temporary film studio.

The green structure is surrounded by blue awnings, caravans, wooden boards and mud. There are piles of film-set paraphernalia tucked under heavy plastic, weighed down with car tyres. There are lorries everywhere, with open backs, as equipment is being manhandled on and off.

But inside the former cowshed, which is used as one of the Isle of Man locations for half the filming schedule, the scene is transformed. This is the Potter household, *circa* 1905. So there is the splendid front door of what appears to be a house, a staircase which leads to nowhere, plus a drawing room and dining room. There is also a conservatory, through a set of French windows.

The drawing room is set for a Christmas scene, in which the Potters entertain. A real tree stands in the corner, covered in candles and decorations; presents of the day, like a toy trumpet, surround the base. On the mantelpiece and sideboards, there is an array of genuine Christmas cards from the period, some with their messages of good cheer scrawled on the back. There is a large bowl of boiled sweets, Faberge eggs, bowls of nuts, a dinner gong with the date 1897, and paintings of actors Bill Paterson and Barbara Flynn, playing Beatrix's parents, Rupert and Helen Potter, in their full, splendid Edwardian dress.

ABOVE *Millie Warne (Emily Watson) at the Potters' Christmas party*

BELOW *Mr and Mrs Potter (Bill Paterson and Barbara Flynn)*

It is unlikely that any of this backdrop, all laid out on genuine furniture of the late Victorian or early Edwardian era, will be really noticed by audiences watching the film. But the attention to detail makes the actors feel as if they are in an authentic setting. In the dining room, lined with tartan wallpaper in keeping with the fashion of the time, there are glass candelabra, cut glasses, remnants of cheese and cigars, glass ashtrays and condiments on giant sideboards.

There is even a printed dinner menu, which consists of mulligatawny soup, potted cheese, a pigeon pie, pigs' feet with truffles, boiled turkey with quails and celery sauce, partridges with roast hares, mince pies, orange jelly, lemon cream, plum pudding, and nuts and cheeses. A visitor to the set had caused some hilarity the day before, when she asked, 'Where did you find a house like this?' She was so taken in with the atmosphere, she assumed that the cowshed had been constructed over the house itself, to protect it from the wind and rain.

It is in this space that Renée Zellweger delivers many of the key scenes. And the scene today, Wednesday, April 5th, 2006, is one between Beatrix and Norman's sister, Millie (Emily Watson), who has become a close friend. Beatrix is about to deliver the news that Norman has asked her to marry him.

Here is this section of the original script – and what happened in the delivery of the words. It is fairly typical of most scenes in *Miss Potter*, as director and stars make it work for the screen.

ABOVE *Dinner is served*

BELOW *Millie and Norman (Emily Watson and Ewan McGregor)*

INT. CONSERVATORY, POTTER HOUSE – NIGHT

BEATRIX leads MILLIE into the conservatory, overlooking the garden, where they can speak alone.

MILLIE: What is it? Is there something wrong?

BEATRIX: Oh, no, but as my confidante . . .

MILLIE: You have something to confide? How delicious!

BEATRIX: We're happy with our lot, aren't we, Millie?

MILLIE: What lot is that?

BEATRIX: Being unmarried. We're free. Free of the burdens that drag down other women.

MILLIE: Yes, it's a blessing from God. A secret blessing, but a blessing nevertheless. Has something happened? You've gone puce, my dear.

BEATRIX: Your brother has asked me to marry him.

MILLIE: Norman?!

BEATRIX: And I feel quite irrationally that I . . . may accept.

Take Five – in the Back of the Cowshed

MILLIE: You and my brother!

BEATRIX: I want your approval.

MILLIE: My approval! Beatrix, marry him! Tomorrow! Don't waste a moment! How can you hesitate?

BEATRIX: You don't hate me?

MILLIE: For God's sake, why would I hate you?

BEATRIX: Both Norman and me. It would leave you alone.

MILLIE: You have a chance for happiness, Beatrix, and you're worrying about me! I wouldn't worry about you. If someone came along who loved me and whom I loved, I'd trample over my mother. You love Norman? Marry him! Don't you dare think about anyone else!

BEATRIX: What about the blessings of spinsterhood?

MILLIE: Hogwash! What else is a woman alone supposed to say? You have a chance to be loved! Take it! Leave me to be happy knowing the two people I love are happy. That's the most thought you should ever have for me.

HELEN POTTER appears at the door.

HELEN: Our guests are leaving, Beatrix. Come and see them out.

BEATRIX: Of course, mother. I love you, Millie.

ABOVE *Barbara Flynn as Mrs Potter*

BELOW *Production designer Martin Childs*

The actresses, both dressed in high-necked blouses and long skirts, with hair pinned back, are ready to go and the scene is set.

'Shooting . . . turn over. And . . . action!'

The clapperboard is snapped: Scene 260. Take 1.

The lines are delivered faultlessly, but there is a clumsy entrance with the door to the conservatory. They will have to go again. Also, the actors want to take out lines to make the scene move faster. They decide to drop Beatrix asking, 'We're happy with our lot, aren't we, Millie?' and all the lines up to 'You've gone puce', going straight to 'Your brother has asked me to marry him.' The director agrees.

Production designer Martin Childs is watching a re-run of the scene on a nearby monitor. He suddenly notices that someone has left a cloth draped over a wicker table. 'That cloth should not be there,' he says. 'The table should be bare.' But there is no time to remove it before the next take.

The Making of Miss Potter

Take 2.

Again, they are word perfect. But a tree obscures part of the scene. They need a mark on the wooden floor, so they can stand in the right place. As the mark is made, a relieved Childs swoops in, takes off the cloth and checks that the table is in the right place for the scene.

Another take.

Watson freezes as she is about to ask, 'Norman?'

'Bugger,' she says.

She decides that it will be best to indicate her surprise with her eyes and manner, rather than declare his name or deliver the line, 'You and my brother!'

Another take.

Word perfect, picture perfect. And the director's seal of approval: 'Check the gate.'

The gate is the aperture, through which film speeds at ninety feet a minute. It sometimes becomes smeared with dust during a scene, or a hair, unaccountably, is trapped in it. If that is the case, they have to go again.

This time the gate is clear and the master shot is completed.

ABOVE *Director Chris Noonan, script supervisor Sue Hills and Renée Zellweger study the monitor. Director of photography Andrew Dunn is back left*

BELOW *Checking the camera gate*

Take Five – in the Back of the Cowshed

There then follows a sequence in which director Noonan films Zellweger's close-up, while Watson acts opposite her. The lines are the same.

Now the takes mount up. Each one sounds good to the untrained ear, but director and actresses work tirelessly on a seemingly endless variety of nuance in tone and expression.

Out of sight of the actors, a group of crew members, who have been up since 5 a.m. setting up the Christmas table scene, play silent rope-knotting tricks.

At last, a take that seems to satisfy all the participants. But now there is a rumbling noise in the background.

The sound man declares, 'There was a plane overhead – it sounds like the Battle of Britain.'

They go again with another take. This time Emily Watson instinctively kisses Zellweger's cheek on the final line, 'I love you, Millie.' It looks natural and seems to work. The director suggests that they use it again.

They do so. Perfect take. Perfect timing. Check the gate . . .

OPPOSITE *Beatrix (Renée Zellweger) is in love*

ABOVE *Getting ready to shoot*

BELOW *Sound mixer Peter Lindsay*

Take Five – in the Back of the Cowshed

Chapter Three

RENÉE ZELLWEGER'S LOVE AFFAIR WITH MISS POTTER

'When I studied the script, I began to feel the character and recognize who she might have been.'

BIRTHS

On Saturday, the 28th inst. at 2, Bolton Gardens, South Kensington, the wife of RUPERT POTTER Esq., barrister-at-law, of a daughter.

This simple notice in *The Times* on Monday, July 30th, 1866, announced the arrival of Beatrix Potter, destined to become one of the world's most successful female children's authors. Ironically, her mother, Helen, was not named in the announcement.

That is how notices were written at the time among what were then known as the upper middle-class families of England. Women were treated as second-class citizens, whatever income group they belonged to.

Beatrix was to become a highly successful independent woman. But it took her until middle age to establish herself, in the eyes of her critical parents – and herself.

Here are some of the key dates and moments in her life:

July 25th, 1905: Beatrix accepts a marriage proposal at the age of 38, from Norman Warne, the youngest of publisher Frederick Warne's three sons. Norman died of leukaemia, aged 37, exactly one month later, on August 25th.

November, 1905: Beatrix purchases Hill Top, a working farm in the village of Near Sawrey in the Lake District. Her grandparents, on both sides of the family, made their fortunes from the Lancashire cotton mills. She declared that, despite her London upbringing, her 'interests and joy' belonged to the north country. She was eventually to buy fifteen farms.

October 15th, 1913: Beatrix marries solicitor William Heelis at St Mary Abbot's parish church in Kensington, London. She was 47. He was 42.

1914: Beatrix's father, Rupert Potter, dies at the age of 82.

1918: Beatrix's only brother, Bertram, dies at the age of 46.

1919: Beatrix buys Lindeth Howe in Storrs, Windermere, for her mother, Helen Potter.

December 20th, 1932: Beatrix's mother, Helen, dies, aged 93.

DEATHS

On Wednesday, December 22nd, 1943, at Castle Cottage, Sawrey, near Ambleside, HELEN BEATRIX, dearly beloved wife of WILLIAM HEELIS, and only daughter of the late Rupert Potter. Cremation private. No mourning, no flowers and no letters, please.

The Making of Miss Potter

The Beatrix Potter books

(Published by F. Warne & Co. unless otherwise stated)

The Tale of Peter Rabbit (privately printed)	*1901*
The Tale of Peter Rabbit	*1902*
The Tailor of Gloucester (privately printed)	*1902*
The Tale of Squirrel Nutkin	*1903*
The Tailor of Gloucester	*1903*
The Tale of Benjamin Bunny	*1904*
The Tale of Two Bad Mice	*1904*
The Tale of Mrs. Tiggy-Winkle	*1905*
The Pie and The Patty-Pan	*1905*
The Tale of Mr. Jeremy Fisher	*1906*
The Story of A Fierce Bad Rabbit	*1906*
The Story of Miss Moppet	*1906*
The Tale of Tom Kitten	*1907*
The Tale of Jemima Puddle-Duck	*1908*
The Roly-Poly Pudding	
later renamed The Tale of Samuel Whiskers	*1908*
The Tale of The Flopsy Bunnies	*1909*
The Tale of Ginger and Pickles	*1909*
The Tale of Mrs. Tittlemouse	*1910*
Peter Rabbit's Painting Book	*1911*
The Tale of Timmy Tiptoes	*1911*
The Tale of Mr. Tod	*1912*
The Tale of Pigling Bland	*1913*
Tom Kitten's Painting Book	*1917*
Appley Dapply's Nursery Rhymes	*1917*
The Tale of Johnny Town-Mouse	*1918*
Cecily Parsley's Nursery Rhymes	*1922*
Jemima Puddle-Duck's Painting Book	*1925*
Peter Rabbit's Almanac for 1929	*1928*
The Fairy Caravan (David McKay, Philadelphia)	*1929*
The Tale of Little Pig Robinson	*1930*

Beatrix and Renée

ABOVE *Beatrix
visits the publishers,
Frederick Warne
& Co., to discuss
the publication
of her stories*

RIGHT *Miss Wiggin
(Matyelok Gibbs)*

When she started researching the role, Renée Zellweger became intrigued by the real Beatrix Potter, an artistic woman of her own age living in London, exactly one century before. There was such a marked contrast between expectations then and now.

'I found it remarkable that during her friendship with Norman Warne, Beatrix was never alone with him,' she says. 'She always had a chaperone, even though she was a woman in her late thirties. If she went to Norman's house, his sister Millie was always there. Yet they were able to get to know each other well enough for him to want to propose to her – and for her to want to accept.'

In reality, Norman wrote his proposal by letter. But for the purpose of the dramatic content of the film,

Norman does propose face-to-face. Yet the pressure her parents successfully wielded to keep the engagement a secret is strictly followed in the film's script.

The film uses an ever-present character, the imperious Miss Wiggin (played by 73-year-old Matyelok Gibbs), as a mostly silent chaperone. Dressed in black, with a constantly grim expression, she illustrates the restriction that Beatrix was under every time she tried to have a light or social conversation.

Part of what fascinated Zellweger was the mystery of Miss Potter's personality. 'I knew so little about her, because she was so determined to maintain the integrity of her private life,' Zellweger says, with clear admiration. 'The more I read and the more information I was given, the more uncertain I became about who she really might have been.

'She talked in her diaries about privacy and not wanting to be known. There is also no known record of her speaking voice, even though she must have been in such demand to talk. It made a very interesting journey for me to find the best way to be accurate and to put the pieces of the puzzle together.

'The people closest to her described her as merry, joyful and jolly. She had a glow, apparently, with laughing eyes of brilliant blue. But there are so many contradictions. On the one hand she appears to have been outgoing and expressive, and

yet it seems sometimes she was very introverted and felt discomforted in crowds.

'But when I studied the script, I began to feel the character and recognize who she might have been. I began to understand why her growing up informed the woman she became. I understood why she became more reserved because of the restrictions placed on her by her parents.

'She was cut off from her peers, from the people who you would normally expect her to move around. She was also insecure. It made perfect sense to me – why she needed these characters, from Peter Rabbit onwards, to express things she could not say. It is clear she had a very rich internal existence.

'I can understand her move to the Lake District and wanting to set up a new life for herself. She had become well known before settling there. I can understand the appeal of wanting to be distanced from the exchanges you have every day as a public person. I understand why you would want to go somewhere more remote, so your exchanges are less public. Particularly if you are someone who is introverted and cherishes privacy.'

OPPOSITE *Beatrix rides in her carriage through Hyde Park*

ABOVE *Filming the carriage with a tracking vehicle*

BELOW *Renée Zellweger with other cast members at 'The World of Beatrix Potter Attraction'*

The internationally-acclaimed actress and the late world-famous author certainly have in common a love of privacy. And for such a publicly known actress, Zellweger remains shy. A surprisingly high number of actors are self-conscious when not in character.

It showed in her case when, during the Lake District filming, she was invited as guest of honour to 'The World of Beatrix Potter Attraction' in Bowness-on-Windermere. She attended an unveiling of a sculpture by Anthony Bennett, where it was hoped she would take centre-stage at some point. But she slipped on her dark glasses and preferred to remain on the fringes of the ceremony for much of the time.

'I do my best, but I am really not very good at these things,' she said. 'I always admire people who can be extrovert and confident. I *can* be confident, but I like it to be among people I know well. I cannot instantly relax in new company, although it may sometimes seem that I can. I am not a "look at me!" girl.'

But millions of cinema audiences have taken a good look at Zellweger and like what they

The Making of Miss Potter

see. Just twelve years ago she was playing characters like Starlene Cheatham in the film with the torturous title, *Love and a .45* or Tami in *Reality Bites*. But her role as the loyal Dorothy Boyd alongside Tom Cruise's frantic sports agent in *Jerry Maguire* acted as a rocket-booster to her career. She was able to win lead roles in the likes of *A Price Above Rubies* (with Britain's Chris Eccleston) and the comedy *Nurse Betty* (with Morgan Freeman), before landing the female lead in Jim Carrey's 2000 film *Me, Myself & Irene*. Then came *Bridget Jones's Diary* and she suddenly received wide recognition.

She is repeating her acting method, used in two Bridget Jones films, of maintaining her English accent at all times. She does not even break into her native Texan accent, which is relaxed and warm, when talking to her friends on her mobile telephone. However Texans have a reputation for being open and friendly and, even within the self-imposed limitations of filming schedules and

acting discipline, Zellweger certainly shows these characteristics. She is popular with the crew.

So is her acting career how she hoped it would be, when she took her first faltering steps after university in Texas? And are there any regrets that she left her home to seek better and bigger roles in Los Angeles?

'I never realised how important this medium would become to me as a creative outlet,' she says. 'I knew that I'd gravitated towards it, naturally, since I was really young. When I moved to Los Angeles, it was fantastic and terrifying. It was a magnificent adventure, which I found liberating. I felt like a cultural voyeur – even though my working life was mostly spent behind a bar, serving drinks or clearing up. But through this profession I have learned so much and been given the most extraordinary opportunities. The opportunity to play Beatrix Potter is a perfect example.'

The voice of Beatrix: from Katy to Kensington

Renée Zellweger, brought up in small-town Katy, Texas, has had to transform her accent to a woman raised in the rarefied atmosphere of South Kensington, London, at the turn of the last century.

She has had dialect coach Barbara Berkery at her side, every day, to help make sure there are no mistakes. Berkery, well known for twice helping Gwyneth Paltrow in *Emma* (1996) and *Sliding Doors* (1998), plus Zellweger in both Bridget Jones performances, listens to every take, every day.

Even if Zellweger slips up in a take which has no hope of being used, Berkery reminds her of the right vowels. But the actress rarely makes an error, remaining in character with her voice throughout filming.

But the moment filming is over on the final day, she talks in her own voice. The instant return to her sing-song Texan comes as a surprise to all the film crew who have not worked with her before. The same thing happened on *Bridget Jones*.

'Every actor has a different approach,' says Berkery. 'Gwyneth Paltrow or Geoffrey Rush, who I've also worked with, will only use their accents in front of the cameras. With Renée, she never drops it until the film is over.'

ABOVE & OPPOSITE Beatrix Potter the artist and props from the studio

BELOW Dialect coach Barbara Berkery

But Berkery is the first to admit that she is having to make a calculated guess at Beatrix Potter's real voice. She is also softening it from how it would have sounded.

'It is likely to have been quite tight and she would probably have had a high voice,' says Berkery. 'She would have probably spoken in a way we would now regard as posh. The dresses and manners of the day also pushed up the sound of the voice.

'That would have grated on the audience during the film and it would have become irritating. So we have kept the voice reasonably soft, but just made the consonants sharp and clean and the vowels slightly clipped.'

It is also a very different voice from Zellweger's version of Bridget Jones. 'Bridget's was specifically a media accent, that of a Home Counties girl going into the media. It was slightly slushy, particularly with the t's and d's. But even if we do not have a recording of Beatrix Potter, we have a good idea of how she would have sounded by the end of the 19th century.

Renée Zellweger's Love Affair with Miss Potter

ABOVE *Barbara Berkery*

OPPOSITE *Beatrix (Renée Zellweger) waits anxiously for Norman*

'What we call RP – received pronunciation – started around the 1850s. It was a time when Britain ran an empire. It was also the flowering of the public schools which sent pupils out to careers in the empire. Before that, accents were much more regional. Even in Shakespeare, with Hotspur, who was from the north-east, there is a line saying his voice goes up and down. He was an unashamed Geordie.

'Beatrix, despite her northern grandparents, was brought up by her social-climbing mother. Mrs Potter would have concentrated on making her daughter speak rather like the upper class of the day. Beatrix's family was from the new middle class which wanted to copy.'

Berkery is a former actress, trained at RADA, who is now one of the premier voice coaches. She has coached actors like Brad Pitt (*Seven Years in Tibet*, 1997) and Natalie Portman for the 2006 film, *V for Vendetta*.

'Whenever I start with a new actor, I take them through voice placement,' she says. 'The West Country accent is more at the back of the throat. The Belfast accent, for example, is placed forward. If actors have an affinity for language, it is easy. If they are word-blunted, it is going to be more difficult.'

The next lesson is the actual sound. 'It is where you make the sounds in the mouth,' she says. 'If you think of a general American accent, the mouth is broad. Scottish is tight. If it is Lancashire, the mouth is very busy. They used to mouth words across the racket of the mills. In Devon, there used to be many men of the sea. The mouth seems to reflect that glare of the sea, somehow. In Norfolk, the voice is very flat.

'The actor Bernard Hepton, who was brilliant at accents, famously said that the Australian accent was mostly cockney. But the sun was suddenly in their eyes in Australia and the voice became stretched.'

Berkery applies the same rules to all actors. 'You do not frighten them by asking for too much, too soon,' she says. 'Fortunately, Renée is very bright and understood the whole thing from the start. I think it also helped that she has European parents (Swiss father, Norwegian mother) and that made her more flexible.

'I am always concerned that Americans may be very stiff with an English accent and their natural acting ability is hurt by that. But with Renée, she seems to do it with ease. The way she sheds the accent like a coat the moment the last scene is filmed makes me think that it is like everything with her – total dedication.'

The Making of Miss Potter

Chapter Four

THE SUITORS

❧

Ewan McGregor:
Trainspotting *to a* **Victorian Gentleman**

'*This is what you are always looking for in acting – a chance to play someone who is completely different.*'

Ewan McGregor is suited and booted in unfamiliar black frock coat, acting nervously. He is playing publisher Norman Warne who is calling on Beatrix Potter for the first time and he's working himself up to be sufficiently stumbling and bumbling. He knocks on the front door and is introduced, stuttering his words as he does so.

McGregor, in the Aladdin's cave of a cowshed on the Isle of Man which has been transformed as the sumptuous interior for the Potter household, is clearly in his element. He has grown a moustache identical to Warne's and sleeked down his usual fair hair in a severe parting. 'I saw the cracking moustache in the old photographs and decided to go for it,' he tells me, between takes.

He strikes a handsome figure as he strides across the film set, only to appear stooped and humbled at his meeting with Zellweger's Beatrix.

'A lot of thought and preparation goes into every scene,' he says. 'I thought of this as a first business meeting when he wants to publish her book, *The Tale of Peter Rabbit*. I am sure his brothers said something on the lines of, "This Miss Potter is a right piece of work and a tough cookie." They put the fear of God into him. So he is quite nervous and clumsy. I have to strike the right balance. There are a lot of nice moments later when you see them falling in love and becoming more comfortable with each other as he grows in confidence.'

The next time McGregor delivers the scene, he stumbles as he leaves, making Zellweger roar with laughter. I thought it was a mistake, until I checked the script (see page 59, 'The First Meeting'). He is supposed to lose his footing slightly on the doorstep; but he makes it so natural, grabbing at a servant's dress only to find that his hand lands right on her breasts, that the laughter is unforced.

'That was great,' says Noonan. 'We need to do it again. We just need a brief laugh – ' But Renée is helpless with laughter.

Zellweger is the one of the main reasons that McGregor, 35, star of films as diverse as *Trainspotting* (1996) and *Moulin Rouge* (2001), is now dressed in black and clutching a top hat. They had co-starred in a 2003 film, *Down with Love*. 'It was supposed to be a comedy, 1960s style,' says McGregor. 'We were like Rock Hudson and Doris Day, wearing glamorous clothes and living the life of Hollywood studio actors of forty or fifty years ago. If you did not get it absolutely right, it did not work. We kept on saying. "Let's do something straightforward together – something not so technical or tricky."'

McGregor describes Miss Potter's personal love story as 'desperate'. She was a woman in her late thirties, who had shrugged off suitors lined up by her parents. She concentrated only on her work. 'So I thought there must be something special about Norman,' he says. 'He spends a lot of time in the company of women – his mother or sister and their female friends – and he is probably quite good with them. And I have a feeling he was already hooked by Beatrix's work and I think he's thrilled with her. He can't have imagined he would be with such a fantastic woman, working with her. So I think he falls for her very quickly – long before she falls for him.'

There was a point in the research when the actor himself was similarly smitten.

'I went to see her work at an exhibition in Dulwich Art Gallery, out of a sense of duty,' he says. 'But I was really taken with it. When you see her animals, they are divine, really tiny, detailed little watercolours. They are still animals, though, even if they are wearing coats. There is a special quality to them which is instantly appealing.'

McGregor, a family man, is also surrounded by Miss Potter at home. 'Our house is full of Potter stuff – and I hadn't even noticed,' he says. 'My parents sent the complete works for the children and we have books, egg cups, plates – the

lot. Beatrix Potter has become something of an institution without many of us knowing. When I read the script, I realised what an extraordinary woman she really was.'

This role is a complete change of pace for McGregor (who also enjoys the irony of sharing a name with Beatrix Potter's own infamous character Mr McGregor). He likes to live on the razor's edge of acting. Ask him to do something he hasn't tried before and he will give it a go. Clothes on, clothes off, tailored toff or down-and-out, singer, dancer or *Star Wars* hero, he's done the lot. So he is excited with his role as a gentleman from a century ago and the approach by director Chris Noonan.

'Chris got us together and set up a lovely day before the start,' he says. 'He got us to talk about the characters. We didn't do a conventional script read-through, which is a complete waste of time. At first, I thought, "How can we do this, when we have not even started filming?" I was thinking, "God, I don't know what I am going to say when it comes to me." But, suddenly, I found that I had a lot of understanding for the part, which I had not realised.'

Directors sometimes use such game-playing methods to establish who are the strongest characters, both on and off screen. That was true of Matyelok Gibbs, a 73-year-old veteran who plays the silent Miss Wiggin. 'She had the longest, most intricate story about her character,' says McGregor. 'On the page, she's just this grumpy lady. But Matyelok invented so much detail on her, it was incredible. Everyone noticed and her part was given an extra dimension by Chris.'

ABOVE *Ewan McGregor as Norman Warne*

OPPOSITE TOP
Beatrix and Norman take tea together. Director Chris Noonan discusses the scene with Renée Zellweger and Ewan McGregor

OPPOSITE BOTTOM
Focus puller Mark Millsome measures the next shot for focus

The Suitors

The extra dimension brought by Renée Zellweger, though, was less expected. She decided to talk in an English accent – and kept it throughout the filming. McGregor delivers Norman Warne in the well-spoken English which would have certainly been true of his character at the time. But he switches back to his native Scottish accent the minute the scene is over.

Most of McGregor's clothes were off-the-peg from the original old collections at London costumiers, Cosprop. 'The clothes play a massive part, because, physically, I hold myself differently,' he says. 'You cannot slouch around, because you're in a starched collar. And the women are in corsets. So you sit and stand in a rather formal manner. You cannot help it. And you can imagine how Norman might have stood, walked and talked.'

McGregor certainly walks the walk and talks the talk as Norman, who becomes more assured in each scene with Beatrix. The key romantic scene is a kiss at a railway station. 'It was a lovely scene, but I never learn,' he says. 'When I see a scene which says, "Exterior, rain",

The Making of Miss Potter

shooting in March in England, I ought to know that it is going to be cold and miserable.

'I said to Anthony Powell, the costume designer, "Can't I put glycerine on the clothes, to make them look wet without being wet?" He just laughed. So I was sprayed – regularly – to make me drenched. On the final day of filming that sequence, it was even snowing. It was one of my coldest experiences on any film set. But it is the nearest thing you get to a sex scene in the entire movie – and it is far more powerful as a result.'

McGregor has enjoyed a series of major roles in recent years, whether with upcoming star Scarlett Johansson in *The Island* (2005) or one of the most established stars, Nicole Kidman, in *Moulin Rouge*. He has delivered a wide range of films like *Shallow Grave*, *A Life Less Ordinary*, *Velvet Goldmine*, *Little Voice* and *Young Adam*. But *Moulin Rouge*, the esoteric *Big Fish* and *Star Wars* have made him a name in Hollywood. His assured performance as Norman Warne yet again proves why he is one of a handful of British stars who in the last ten years have been able to sell themselves to America.

"Fame is a strange situation because in one sense it is what you strive for and then, when it's there, it can be quite difficult. People I meet for the first time already have ideas about who I am and what I'm like. The way I deal with it is that if I get on with them I do, and if I don't, I don't. Otherwise, you can drive yourself nuts.'

It is clear that McGregor is anything but nuts. Beneath the banter, there's a touch of the poet about him. He weaves his descriptions well, with directness and honesty.

It is probably a complete contrast to how Norman Warne and Beatrix Potter would have spoken to each other. 'He would have been shy and awkward and I am sure she was careful about what she said,' he asserts.

'But this is what you are always looking for in acting – a chance to play someone who is completely different. The nice thing about my job is that the more I go on, the more I get the chance to work with people I've always wanted to work with. I enjoy being an actor more each day. It is the chance to explore characters like Norman which make it so enjoyable.'

OPPOSITE TOP
Norman Warne (Ewan McGregor) at home

OPPOSITE BOTTOM
Creating a rain-splashed train

ABOVE *Sopping wet in the driving rain, Norman (Ewan McGregor) arrives at the station to see Beatrix off*

The Making of Miss Potter

The Man Beatrix Married: Lloyd Owen as William Heelis

Lloyd Owen makes his *Miss Potter* debut on a steep and stony path, clinging to a hill, overlooking the still sheen of Lake Grasmere, in the heart of the Lake District. The dead calm is broken only by the distant burble of running water from one of the streams which penetrate the sheer slopes. On this spring day the countryside is emerging, green and fresh, from the hundreds of acres of brown hillside, in which winter frosts have etched deep. But there is much tension in the clear air and no time to enjoy the views or the moment.

Owen, 40, is having to shed the years for a scene, set in 1881, with a young actress who is playing Beatrix aged 16, on a visit with her parents to the Lakes. 'There, Miss Beatrix,' he announces, waving to the landscape around him. 'The miracle of the English countryside. Lush. Ripe. Doesn't it just explode with energy?'

There begins a scene, repeated several times. In between, the six-foot two-inch tall Owen munches anxiously on an apple. A make-up girl complains of being giddy at the height. One of the crew, a grip, had earlier in the day broken an ankle by going over on the stony path. This is an edgy, nervous day. Film sets often become like this after a time, particularly those which are running for twelve-hour days on six-day weeks. A tiredness and irritability sets in. It is difficult to keep up the energy levels.

OPPOSITE *Beatrix Potter (Renée Zellweger) and Norman Warne (Ewan McGregor) become better acquainted*

ABOVE *Country solicitor William Heelis (Lloyd Owen) advises Beatrix about purchasing property in the Lake District*

Director Chris Noonan remains uncertain about the scene. Is it needed for the film? Will it work to see an actress play a young Beatrix and actor Owen pretending to be a young Heelis? Do they look right together? Will a cinema audience be confused? (The scene was in fact cut from the film and reshot later, using Justin McDonald as the young William.)

The next day, April 22nd, 2006, the mood has not changed much. Owen has to age up to meet the older Beatrix, played by Zellweger of course, a few years after Norman Warne's sudden death. The scene is supposed to be Castle Farm, which Beatrix bought in 1909. The film crew is creating an Edwardian hill farm in a new location, a prelude to the final scene in the film. The weather has turned cold and grey on what should be a bright, blue morning.

Owen knows that he is under pressure. He is the last major actor to arrive on a film set, with which the other cast members and crew are now familiar.

'Am I nervous?' he asks. 'Yes, I am certainly on edge. There are moments when you are talking to a well-known actress like Renée, when your mind is thinking, "Here I am, talking to Renée Zellweger!" and your brain is not properly taking in what she is saying.

'That only lasts for a short time. I am here to do a job and have to make sure I do it well. I am not always happy with my performance. At one point, when the director was ready to move on, Renée said, "You want to do another take, don't you?" I felt that I had not properly achieved what I had wanted, so she made sure we went again.'

Owen, trained at the prestigious Royal Academy of Dramatic Art – RADA for short – is not a high-flying star. He has been a solid working actor, who has enjoyed flashes of recognition through the television series *Monarch of the Glen* (playing Paul Bowman-MacDonald) and *The Young Indiana Jones Chronicles* (Professor Henry Jones, Sr). His working life has varied between TV slots, theatre tours and spells at the National Theatre.

He has an appealing attitude towards acting. 'I have been with some well-known actors on TV, who think that they are bigger than the part,' he says. 'When an assistant director gets an umbrella for them when it's raining, they think it is for them – rather than to keep dry the costume that they are wearing.'

His TV work is quite a contrast to what he's been asked to deliver in *Miss Potter*, his first major film. He must be struggling to adapt, but remains strong and confident. His Westmorland accent and old-world, gentlemanly behaviour and manner seem spot-on.

OPPOSITE Lloyd Owen as William Heelis

ABOVE Between shots Lloyd Owen shares conversation with producers David Kirschner and Arnie Messer

BELOW William Heelis (Lloyd Owen) and Beatrix (Renée Zellweger) set off for a walk

'I think the director was under pressure to cast a well-known actor,' he says. 'But I am delighted that he went for me. I felt that I knew the sort of man William Heelis would have been.' The London-based Owen, son of the late actor Glyn Owen, also felt that he knew what he calls 'the English northern sensibilities' through his Welsh-born father, who was brought up in Bolton, Lancashire.

'There is a feeling in London and the south that everyone up north speaks with a flat accent and there is no sense of snobbery about them,' he says. 'That is not true. Although Beatrix's parents thought William wasn't suitable for their daughter, the Heelis family had been land agents, pastors and lawyers in what used to be called Westmorland (now Cumbria) for four hundred years and they looked down on the Potters.'

Owen, who has a fifteen-year-old son and eight-year-old daughter, has painstakingly researched his role. He contacted surviving members of the Heelis family. There are no direct descendants from William Heelis, who had no children with Beatrix. 'But I did find family members, like Guy Heelis, who is still working as a land agent,' he says. 'The family has bought and sold the same land in this area since 1565. I've got the family tree at home and it's absolutely enormous. When they look at the deeds, they can see

The Making of Miss Potter

their ancestors from four hundred years ago. So the Heelis family is very established in this area.'

He also traced George Crossley, aged 92, who as a teenage clerk worked in the solicitor's office of William Heelis during the 1930s. 'It is an interesting insight into working and public behaviour,' he relates. 'Each morning, when their boss came in, they would all stand and say, "Good morning, sir." After that, they were allowed to call him Mr Heelis. Then every day Beatrix arrived in a chauffeur-driven car. She would turn to Mr Crossley and ask, "Hello, George – is my husband in?" He always was, so she went to see him in the office for a time. She then departed in her chauffeur-driven car to take charge of her farms.'

Owen has been able to form a clear view on the kind of man he is playing. 'It seems a dreadful generalisation, but men in marriage either keep their heads down or put them above the parapet,' he says. 'William, from what I can tell, definitely kept his down. He got on with playing his golf and bowls. He also smoked like a chimney, apparently. The fireplace in his office was full of cigarettes, every day.

'But, despite being a keen sportsman, he was not allowed a radio by Beatrix. So he used to have to phone up George Crossley to find out the latest cricket scores. She obviously ruled the roost. And when he went fishing, it was Beatrix who rowed the boat. It was as if she was in charge.'

An image comes across of a woman who was also very cautious about spending her money on frivolities. She even regarded electricity with the greatest suspicion. According to George Crossley (who also reported that William was a "terrible driver") she insisted that they have oil lamps at their home – yet allowed electricity to be used in barns, for the animals.

'William was married to a highly successful woman whose book royalties allowed her to buy all her farms and successfully breed sheep,' says Owen. 'But she was never really known as Beatrix Potter, the author. She always signed herself "Mrs William Heelis" or "Beatrix Heelis" and did not talk about her old life.

'I did not need this information to act, but it gave me an insight into the mood and atmosphere of the time. I felt that, on this, every little helped. You never see this extra information on screen, but it all adds to the mixture.'

The Suitors

Chapter Five

THE TROUBLED BEATRIX POTTER FILM

——✦——

'When Renée Zellweger is in front of the camera and the director calls "Action!" then I will believe it.'

The Writer: Richard Maltby, Jr

The long trail to bring Beatrix Potter to the screen started by chance in 1992, more than 3,000 miles from where she lived and died. Richard Maltby, Jr, lyricist and Tony Award-winning director of hit Broadway musicals like *Ain't Misbehavin'*, was taking a break in a luxurious hotel, the Homestead, in the Blue Ridge Mountains of Virginia.

'Looking for something to read to my children, ages 3 and 1, I found a book of Beatrix Potter stories on the hotel's bookshelf,' he says. 'On the cover was a brief biography of the author. It said that Beatrix Potter was a spinster in her thirties when she decided to send her children's stories to a publisher, that she fell in love with the publisher and they decided to marry (over her parents objections) – but before there could be a wedding, the man died.'

The biographical details included the fact that she then moved to the Lake District, where she met another man whom she did marry. Maltby reports, 'It said that after this she published virtually no more stories. It was this last sentence that caught my eye. I thought, why? Why, when a writer finally marries happily does she give up writing. One would expect the opposite, that she would write as never before. I was intrigued. I decided to find out more about Beatrix Potter. And from this research came the story of a woman who leaves a fantasy world of her imagination to enter the real world, where she encounters love, great joy and immense tragedy, and who

ultimately chooses to live in reality, with all its harshness, over the safety of her fantasy world.'

It was the start of a long writing and development process for a project which was later to be known in Hollywood trade magazines as 'the troubled Beatrix Potter film'.

Maltby, 67, who adds the Jr title to his name because his father of the same name was a famous American bandleader in the 1950s, initially thought of the story as a musical. He wrote the script on spec, with songs.

Maltby at the time was fresh from receiving a Tony nomination for his lyrics for the hit stage musical *Miss Saigon*. But his long history of success with stage musicals meant nothing in Hollywood. 'Film musicals had gone out of fashion,' he says. 'So I quickly decided to take out the songs.' Maltby also originally envisaged a film with a good deal of animation, like *Mary Poppins*. 'But since the Potter stories are geared to very small children, there was the immediate fear that adults would think it was a children's movie instead of an adult love story, and so step by step the animated sequences were simplified or eliminated.'

In 1994, Maltby showed the script to Cameron Macintosh, who had produced *Song and Dance* and *Miss Saigon* on Broadway. He, in turn, sent it to Channel 4 television. It was then passed on to producer Duncan Kenworthy (later famous for producing *Four Weddings and a Funeral*) who worked for the Jim Henson company in London. 'Duncan was very enthusiastic and we secured a sale,' relates Maltby. It was sold for $25,000, which is around £14,705 at today's rates of $1.7 to the pound.

'I was pleased that the script was in good hands,' says Maltby. 'But, after a while, I was told that Henson wanted to make a lot of changes. The changes proposed did not seem like a good idea, so I offered to buy it back. It cost me $65,000 (£38,235), because they said they had spent a lot of money on preparation. I was not really upset, because the script had sold so quickly at first that I was sure it would sell again immediately.'

It did not sell at all. *Miss Potter* became locked in the glue-like process of being sent to a variety of producers, who all reported that they loved it. 'But they did not love it enough to want to make it,' says Maltby. 'They loved it in the sense that they would read it, enjoy it, then wonder *how* to make it. They loved it in that they offered to employ me to write something else. Or they asked, "What else do you have?" It was a good way to meet people. I had a script that everyone seemed to like, but no one wanted to make.'

Producer David Kirschner, however, took his admiration to the next level. He had begun his career as an illustrator for Jim Henson's Muppet and Sesame Street characters. He had also written

The Making of Miss Potter

and illustrated a series of children's books, *Rose Petal Place*, and had become a children's book collector. But, more importantly, he had created and executive-produced with top director Steven Spielberg the big family hit, *An American Tail* (1986). He had since enjoyed consistent success as an executive producer or producer.

'He worked very hard indeed,' says Maltby. 'He even hooked the interest of Cate Blanchett, who was keen to play Beatrix. But it just did not happen.' Nevertheless, Maltby's loyal long-term agent, Stuart Fry, promised, 'As long as I am an agent, I will be working on this. I am sure, one day, we will get it made.'

Fry attended the 2003 Sundance Film Festival, clutching the script, where he met the young producer, David Thwaites, who was working for former studio head, Mike Medavoy, at Phoenix Pictures. 'Within two days of receiving the script, David called back and said he could make this film,' says Maltby. 'There then began this dance between Cate Blanchett and Renée Zellweger to play Beatrix. Cate dropped out, Renée came in. Then Renée dropped out and Cate came in. Bruce Beresford, the Australian director, had also come in and then *he* dropped out. It was complicated and I thought to myself, I just have to sit back and not get too excited.'

Maltby, in the meantime, was conducting what he calls a 'parallel working life', delivering a musical version of the film *Big*, to Broadway, and directing the Tony Award-winning Broadway production of *Fosse*. 'I could not stand still and wait for this film,' he reasons. 'Even when I met with the film's new director, Chris Noonan, to discuss revisions to the script, I thought, I'm not going to change my life over this. I just hoped that one day the film would be made.'

When David Thwaites telephoned in February 2006, to say that the film's financing was 'closed' (meaning that all financing is in place and contracts are signed), with Renée Zellweger in the role, Maltby remained pragmatic.

'I said, "When Renée Zellweger is in front of the camera and the director calls 'Action!' then I will believe it."'

The Producers: David Kirschner, Mike Medavoy, Corey Sienega, Arnie Messer, David Thwaites

Cate Blanchett, the London-based Australian star actress who had made such an impact as Elizabeth I in the award-winner, *Elizabeth*, in 1998, was the first actress to declare that she wanted to play Beatrix Potter.

She was lined up by producer David Kirschner, who works with business partner Corey Sienega, in Los Angeles. 'I took a scene from *Elizabeth* in which she goes into an alcove, because it seems everyone is plotting against her,' he says. 'There is a portrait of her father, Henry VIII, on the wall, and she looks upset and angry. I added an animated Peter Rabbit coming in to that scene. When Cate first saw it, she started laughing. She also had tears in her eyes, because she knew something of Beatrix's tragic love story.' Blanchett was also keen to work with director Bruce Beresford, a fellow

The Making of Miss Potter

Australian, who had directed films like *Double Jeopardy* and *Evelyn*, with Pierce Brosnan.

However Kirschner, who first consulted with Blanchett in 1999, was in for a shock. His track record, which included executive-producing hits *The Flintstones* (1994) and producing *Hocus Pocus* (1993) did not mean enough. 'I still could not put my financing together immediately to make this film, even with Cate Blanchett,' he recalls. 'It was always going to be a slow process, though, and we were making progress. But she broke my heart a couple of times by leaving the project at key moments.'

The last time was when she took the role of Katherine Hepburn in *The Aviator* (2004), directed by Martin Scorsese. It won her an Oscar for best supporting actress. 'I have become used to surprises and actors coming in and out of projects,' says Kirschner. 'Sometimes, for a variety of reasons, a film does not get made. *Miss Potter* came close to being made with us several times. It was just not to be.'

But in the end the combined determination of producer David Thwaites, his boss Mike Medavoy, and David Kirschner was able to give the project the final push it needed.

Thwaites admits that he knew nothing about Beatrix's personal story. 'I had grown up with her books, of course, and had fond memories of them,' he says. 'So when Richard Maltby's agent, Stuart Fry, told me about the script, I was interested. He said, "You are English. You'll like it." He was right. I gave it to Mike and Arnie Messer, who I work with, and they liked it too.

'From that moment, we tried to make it happen. David Kirschner and Corey Sienega had been working on the project for ten years. The script had gone through many drafts and they had worked on the script alone for about six years before I had seen it. They did all the groundwork. All I did was help prod it along.'

Even so, Thwaites, 30, a former child actor who starred in several television dramas until his late teens, proved a determined negotiator. He opened discussions with Renée Zellweger, through her manager, within weeks of taking on the project.

Cate Blanchett had introduced another Australian director, Chris Noonan, who had been searching for a classy project following his extraordinary success in 1995 with *Babe*. He had rejected many entreaties from Hollywood to make certain movies, refusing on the grounds of poor scripts or his own disinterest.

'I can't tell you how many times either Cate or Renée were going to do it, but it just did not happen,' says Thwaites. 'The most important

OPPOSITE BOTTOM
Producers David Thwaites and David Kirschner with Renée Zellweger outside Hill Top Farm

ABOVE *Producers David Thwaites and Arnie Messer with Renée Zellweger*

BELOW *Renée Zellweger greets producer Mike Medavoy and his son*

thing is to have determination. The film business is full of people who have the power to say no. Very few have the power to say yes and make it happen. If we had stopped every time someone said they did not want to make the film, then it would never have been made.'

It is no secret that other actresses were considered as discussions went on with agents for both Zellweger and Blanchett. American actress Ashley Judd expressed interest. 'There was so much going back and forth on all this,' says Thwaites. 'But we were thrilled that Renée was interested and delighted by her enthusiasm. Ultimately it was her trusting us and committing to the film that got it made.'

Thwaites did not meet her until January 2005. 'I ran into her at a party with her manager, John Carrabino, after the Golden Globes awards,' he says. 'I said, "It is a shame that we never got Potter going." She said, "I loved that script." I said, "Well, it is still around. We can still do it if you commit to it." And she said that she would.'

So finally it was set that Zellweger would star and Noonan would direct. 'The producers met with Renée around April 2005 to talk through the script,' says Thwaites. 'The meeting went on for about five hours. From that point onwards, we have been working towards what we have today.'

The Director: Chris Noonan

Chris Noonan's first discussions with Renée Zellweger took place by email as he was in Sydney and she was in the States. 'But we soon started talking person to person, by phone, and that is when I realised we liked each other. I thought, "Things are going to work out."'

Noonan also noted that Zellweger's film credit as an executive producer was not just window-dressing. 'I asked her who she wanted to play the role of Norman Warne and she suggested Ewan McGregor. Coincidentally, Ewan had also been my first choice for the role,' he reports. 'She had worked with him before (in *Down with Love*, 2003) and she said that there had been a chemistry between them.'

McGregor's agent was approached. 'Getting a star actor into a role can be challenging,' says Noonan. 'There is a courtship which takes place over a certain amount of time. But Renée cut through that just by calling Ewan. He said he liked the thought of doing an awkward character who is bit shy and not sure of himself. So it ended up being fast and straightforward.'

Noonan hired Emily Watson (Millie) next. 'I had approached her about a couple of roles in the past, but they never came to anything,' he says. 'I was not expecting her to accept this role, to be honest, because

OPPOSITE *Renée Zellweger with director Chris Noonan between takes*

ABOVE *Director Chris Noonan rehearses Renée Zellweger and Geoffrey Beavers, who plays Beatrix's bank manager*

BELOW *Assistant director Guy Heeley with camera operator Gerry Vasbenter*

ABOVE *Director Chris Noonan with Emily Watson*

BELOW *Rehearsing the scene in the art gallery – dialect coach Barbara Berkery and Chris Noonan with Renée Zellweger and Emily Watson*

I thought it was too small for her. But she had just had a baby and felt that this was the perfect part for her to come back to work. She is one of my favourite actresses, so I just got lucky.'

Beatrix Potter's parents were also key players. Rupert Potter, who was called to the bar at the age of twenty-three, apparently didn't do a stroke of work for the remainder of his life. He lived in luxury on his grandfather's inheritance, attending his club, the Reform, on most afternoons of the week. But he always gave his daughter a sympathetic ear. Her mother, Helen Potter, was an unashamed social climber. She, separately, had inherited wealth.

'We had to make them very human, despite their social attitudes,' says Noonan. 'It would be very easy to cringe with embarrassment, for example, every time Helen Potter opened her mouth. But our casting director Priscilla John recommended Barbara Flynn (see page 85) to play Helen, with Bill Paterson (see page 82) as Rupert. They were the perfect pair, because they really do seem like a couple. All I could think of, when I heard they'd been hired, was, "This is going to be great."'

Noonan, 54, is friendly, chatty, open, with the natural optimism of an upbeat personality. But for all his easy manner, he is no push-over. 'If it does not work, I say so,' he says. 'It is important to deal with my complaints in the right way. If they haven't got the essence of the scene, it is easier to delay it, send the crew off set, talk about it and work it out. Fortunately, we all share the attitude that if it does not feel real to us, then it won't feel real to an audience, either.'

Noonan cheerfully admits that he was not a big Beatrix Potter fan. 'I did not have any knowledge of her life,' he says. 'I had seen Peter Rabbit on plates and mugs. I dismissed her books as childish little stories.' But he was surprised at what he discovered when he started researching. 'I was astonished to find that there was an extraordinary drama going on in her life.

'I found her to be a standard-bearer for women's rights, without putting those things into strong language. For her sanity, she had to fight for the right to have her stories published – and to marry when she wanted. Women of her class at that time were expected to live their lives on a predetermined course. She said, to hell with the consequences! But we have only a hundred minutes on film to tell that story. That is the challenge.'

ABOVE *Producer David Thwaites works closely with Nigel Wooll (right). As executive producer, Nigel Wooll is responsible for all budgeting and scheduling. The day-to-day logistics of everything from casting to catering are his responsibility and, most crucially from the point of view of the film's backers, he has to ensure the production stays within budget*

Chapter Six

THE TRUE LOVE STORY

The First Meeting

INT. DRAWING ROOM, POTTER HOUSE – DAY

BEATRIX enters the drawing room. She sits on the edge of a chair and adjusts her full skirts. In the background, the noises of a visitor arriving and being greeted. A maid, HILDA, enters.

HILDA: Mr Norman Warne.

He enters. BEATRIX reacts in surprise. MR NORMAN WARNE is not a dour, hairy tradesman like his brothers. He's a handsome young man in his mid-thirties.

MISS WIGGIN, Beatrix's chaperone, enters and sits quietly in a chair in the entry.

NORMAN: Miss Potter, I hope you will forgive my intrusion into your daily routine.

BEATRIX: Oh, I was expecting one of the . . .

NORMAN: I am . . . yes, well, I'm Harold and Fruing's brother. I have recently joined the firm and they have done me the honour of assigning your book to me. It was most gracious of you to invite me to, um . . . to, um . . .

BEATRIX: Tea?

NORMAN: I'd love some. Yes, that would be, um, quite . . . well, yes, thank you. Lemon.

He looks around awkwardly before selecting a seat, begins to sit in the sofa, changes his mind and sits on a chair. BEATRIX watches with some dismay. For the truth is now out: handsome NORMAN WARNE is shy, ill-at-ease, and a bit of a goof.

HELEN POTTER peeks around a corner to spy on them. CUT TO:

INT. DRAWING ROOM, POTTER HOUSE – DAY

Some time later. BEATRIX and NORMAN are looking at BEATRIX'S book.

NORMAN: Extraordinary. Oh! Oh! How funny! (*Giggles as he turns last page*) Delightful! Magical! And so beautifully drawn. Well, I'm . . . well, utterly, utterly speechless.

BEATRIX: Perhaps, Mr Warne, we should discuss our business.

NORMAN: I put your drawings aside with the greatest reluctance.

BEATRIX: Your brother made two proposals which I find quite unacceptable. First, they want the drawings to be in colour. I am adamant they be in black and white.

NORMAN: But . . . Peter Rabbit's blue jacket. And the red radishes. Surely you want your enchanting drawings reproduced as they are?

BEATRIX: Of course I would prefer colour, but colour will make the book cost more than little rabbits can afford. I am adamant. Which brings us to your brothers' second point: they wish to reduce the number of drawings by almost a third. Totally unacceptable.

NORMAN: Miss Potter, let me . . . explain . . . the . . . Oh, I am not good at business. Here is my scheme: if we can reduce the number of drawings to thirty-one precisely, the illustrations for the entire book can be printed on a single sheet of paper, in the, uh what, the three-colour process you desire, and at a reasonable level, of, uh, cost. Yes.

BEATRIX: Oh.

NORMAN: I have given your book a great deal of attention. Truly. I would like it to look colourful on the shelf, so that it stands out from the ordinary books.

The Making of Miss Potter

BEATRIX: My, you have given it some thought. What other books have you supervised?

NORMAN: Personally?

BEATRIX: Yes.

NORMAN: This will be my first.

BEATRIX: Ah.

NORMAN closes the portfolio, and looks up.

NORMAN: Miss Potter, I have recently informed my brothers – and my mother – that I am not content to stay at home and play nursemaid, just because I am the youngest son. I wish to have a proper job in my family's firm. And they have assigned me you. Does that make things clearer?

BEATRIX: I see. In other words, you have no experience whatsoever, but since you've made a nuisance of yourself demanding a chance, they have fobbed you off on me.

NORMAN: Miss Potter, I know only too well what my brothers intended, giving me your 'bunny book', as they call it. But I find your book quite enchanting – delightful! If they intended to 'fob me off', as you say, we shall show them! We are going to give them a bunny book to conjure with! In colours mixed to *your* satisfaction, before your very eyes at the printer.

MISS WIGGIN looks up.

BEATRIX: *(nervous)* At the printer? I could never . . .

NORMAN: I will escort you myself – if you will allow me the honour.

BEATRIX: Why could I never? . . . Of course, I will go. I'm a grown woman. Miss Wiggin will come along. I see no reason why an artist shouldn't visit her printer.

NORMAN rises and bounds towards the door; BEATRIX follows him into the hall.

INT. HALL, POTTER HOUSE – DAY

NORMAN: I shall make all the arrangements. Dear lady, I am . . . in every way . . . uh, what . . . *(He takes her hand)* . . . at your service.

BEATRIX looks at NORMAN's hand holding hers. NORMAN suddenly gets nervous and withdraws it. He realizes that he is still holding her book in the other hand and hands it to her, a bunny painting uppermost. HILDA hands him his coat.

NORMAN (cont): You and rabbits! Extraordinary!

NORMAN leaves. At the step, he turns, walking backwards, trips, and almost falls. BEATRIX, against her judgement, laughs.

The Proposal

UPSTAIRS HALL, POTTER HOUSE – NIGHT

BEATRIX and MISS WIGGIN, in shawls, are waiting on the upstairs hall landing as NORMAN arrives with the coffee.

NORMAN: For you, my dear Miss Wiggin. And you, Miss Potter. (*Whispers to WIGGIN*) I added a little brandy to ours. It is Christmas.

MISS WIGGIN: (*being naughty*) Well, if you promise not to tell . . . (*Takes a sip, tastes the brandy*) Ooooh.

She drinks greedily, then follows NORMAN and BEATRIX past the open door to BEATRIX'S room, where a drawing table is visible.

NORMAN: Is this where you paint, Miss Potter?

BEATRIX: Yes, and this is where we will find your present.

INT. BEATRIX'S ROOM, POTTER HOUSE – NIGHT

They enter the room. MISS WIGGIN stands by the door like a sentry. As NORMAN enters, BEATRIX feels a strange sensation.

BEATRIX: I think – other that Father and Bertram – you're the first man ever to set foot in this room.

NORMAN: Would you like me to . . . leave?

BEATRIX: Of course not. Wiggin is here. And if this is the best I can do for scandal at my age, I'm hardly worthy of my reputation for creativity. Look.

She shows him the watercolour on the table. It depicts a relaxed group of rabbits on the floor roasting apples on a fire, one wearing a scarf similar to one of Norman's scarves.

NORMAN: (*Laughs in delight*) What is it?

BEATRIX: I'm not going to tell you. Not yet.

NORMAN: Ah!

There is a noise. MISS WIGGIN, tipsy and unable to stand, has sunk to a chair beside the door.

BEATRIX: (*showing NORMAN the room*) This is the first drawing I made of Jemima Puddle-duck. I was, what, eight, I think.

NORMAN goes right up to the drawing, almost touching it with his nose, whereupon JEMIMA preens herself, fluttering her eyes flirtatiously at him.

BEATRIX (cont): (*scolding*) Jemima!! Stop that!

NORMAN: (*grinning, suspecting a joke*) Stop what?

JEMIMA waggles her tail at Norman as she turns away.

BEATRIX: Just some silliness.

NORMAN: (*Shrugs it off*) And what's this?

BEATRIX: A music box. My father gave it to me for my sixth birthday. He did the painting on it himself.

NORMAN: So he was an artist too!

BEATRIX: Father always wanted to be an artist. Of course, the family wouldn't hear of it, so he took up law. But the joke is, I've never once heard him discuss a case. He goes to his Club every day, never to his office. I don't really know what he does.

MISS WIGGIN'S coffee cup drops to the floor with a loud clunk. She has fallen asleep on the chair.

NORMAN: Oh dear.

BEATRIX: Wiggin is fallible! Father Christmas lives!

NORMAN: I fear your reputation is now officially dented.

They exchange an awkward smile. Norman looks away, opens the music box. A tinkling melody plays.

NORMAN (*cont*): Ah, very sweet. 'Let Me Teach You How to Dance'. (*beat*) Do you dance, Miss Potter?

BEATRIX: No I don't. Not well.

NORMAN: I make a terrible hash of it when I try, too. But the words are very sweet . . .

BEATRIX: (*winding the box again*) Would you sing it for me?

He shakes his head, mortally embarrassed, but manages to speak in time with the tune as it starts again.

NORMAN: (*awkwardly*) Let me teach you how to dance,
Let me lead you to the floor . . .

She gazes at him, smiling admiringly, encouraging Norman to break into (halting) song. He has a surprisingly pleasant singing voice.

NORMAN (*cont*): SIMPLY PUT YOUR HAND IN MINE
AND THEN THINK OF NOTHING MORE . . .

She adopts a dancing pose, inviting him to join her, and he does so as he continues to sing. Then very slowly and innocently, they dance, in a tiny circle, in the middle of the carpet.

NORMAN (*cont*): LET THE MUSIC CAST ITS SPELL,
GIVE THE ATMOSPHERE A CHANCE,
SIMPLY FOLLOW WHEN I LEAD,
LET ME TEACH YOU HOW TO DANCE.

How can we describe the effect of this moment on BEATRIX? The adolescence that she has never had, the young womanhood that she has never felt, come alive in her. Sensations pass through her body for the first time ever, leaving her breathless and speechless. She looks into NORMAN'S eyes, then looks away.

The music soars on her breathless release of feeling.

NORMAN (*cont*): Miss Potter, I know you have decided not to marry. All my life, I have been confident I would not marry either. But something has happened that has caused me to change my mind.

BEATRIX: Mr Warne!

NORMAN: (*interrupting her*) Please let me go on, for if I don't say what I have to say now, I never will. Miss Potter, I . . . I should like you to consider . . . doing me the honour . . .

BEATRIX, stunned, emits a little squeak.

NORMAN (*cont*): I don't expect an immediate answer.

She tries to speak but cannot.

The Making of Miss Potter

The door swings open and HELEN POTTER enters. BEATRIX and NORMAN are standing at an innocent distance from each other, but the room is definitely full of heat.

HELEN: Beatrix?

BEATRIX: I was showing Mr Warne his Christmas present.

She takes the painting off the table.

BEATRIX (*cont*): I'm an impeccably genteel unmarried lady, Mother. I haven't started to invite men into my room. (*Breezes past her mother*) Come, Mr Warne, it's time for the rest of your present.

NORMAN passes HELEN POTTER and follows BEATRIX into the hall. HELEN POTTER looks at MISS WIGGIN, passed out on the chair.

HELEN: Wiggin!

HELEN POTTER kicks MISS WIGGIN, who wakes with a jolt.

The Kiss

A storm is blowing rain through the gaps above the train on to the covered platforms. As HILDA moves with the POTTERS towards their carriage, we follow SAUNDERS and the PORTERS to the baggage car, where they deposit the luggage.

The POTTERS settle into their compartment, but BEATRIX is distracted. Norman should be here and he isn't. She cranes to search out of the windows.

A man passes by the compartment window and she startles with recognition. She jumps up, grabbing her umbrella and hurries out of the compartment.

HELEN: Beatrix!

BEATRIX leans out of an open door and scans the platform. THERE HE IS! – but walking in the opposite direction. She jumps down and hurries through the rain to catch up to him. She reaches him near the engine, he turns and – alas, it is another man. She deflates and turns back.

MRS POTTER, who has come to the carriage door to investigate, turns back towards the compartment.

A RAILWAY GUARD blows a warning whistle. And behind him appears the real NORMAN, running up the platform towards BEATRIX! With no umbrella, he is dripping wet.

NORMAN: Miss Potter!

BEATRIX: Mr Warne, I was beginning to fear you wouldn't come! You're soaked!

NORMAN: I know, but I wanted to bring the proofs of the new book for your trip.

BEATRIX: Here, share my umbrella. You'll catch a cold.

NORMAN: I couldn't miss seeing you off. You know nothing would stop me.

He blinks rain from his eyes.

BEATRIX: It's going to be the longest summer I've ever spent.

NORMAN: One short summer? What's that? The time isn't for us, it's for them! How can your parents know what's happened to us. They've never felt it. We can afford to give them three months.

The RAILWAY GUARD moves down the platform closing train doors.

BEATRIX: Well, I suppose . . .

Having no other goodbye available, she extends her hand.

NORMAN: This is not how I wish to say goodbye to my fiancée, however . . .

The engine suddenly emits a blast of steam that beclouds the platform and envelops BEATRIX and NORMAN. The two are suddenly alone, swallowed up by this white cloud. Masked by the billowing steam, NORMAN impulsively takes BEATRIX in his arms and kisses her passionately.

The steam dissipates and reveals them standing as before.

NORMAN (*cont*): (*formal, taking her hand*) Goodbye, Miss Potter. I look forward to your swift return.

BEATRIX: (*throbbing from the kiss*) As do I, Mr Warne.

The train begins to move.

NORMAN: Quickly!

BEATRIX hurries and boards the moving train. From the doorway, still shimmering from the unexpected kiss, she waves. It is their first kiss.

BEATRIX: Goodbye, Mr Warne. (*throwing caution away*) Goodbye, Norman!

NORMAN walks with the train, then runs, rain-drenched, until he reaches the end of the platform, and the train pulls away. BEATRIX looks back from the moving train. NORMAN, soaked to the skin and still waving, disappears into the distance.

Chapter Seven

RECREATING HISTORY

>→·—·▷·—◦—·◁·—·←

Anthony Powell: Costume Designer

Anthony Powell was in for a shock when Renée Zellweger viewed his costumes. She didn't like them. 'Or, to be accurate, she loved the look of them – but did not believe that they were right for her to play Beatrix Potter,' he says. 'So about three days before we starting filming, I re-dressed her from scratch. We threw away everything we had done.'

Powell, 71, was not disconcerted by such a blow. The three-time Oscar winner has dressed stars like Harrison Ford, Glenn Close and Sean Connery. 'Renée thought that the clothes we had for her were too pretty and charming,' he says. 'She felt that they should be more boring. It was a bit hair-raising to start all over again in a different direction, but also thrilling and interesting.'

Powell seems in no way hurt or irritated by the last-minute rejection. He is an avuncular man with a big personality, a kindly and hard-working raconteur who is a favourite on set. He has also seen and heard some examples of odd behaviour over the years – even though his lips remained sealed. 'I've worked with some very temperamental people,' he says. 'But, in this case, Renée was not trying to be difficult.

'She had been rehearsing and I could see that the whole thing had suddenly gelled in her mind. She knew who Beatrix was – and it wasn't the sort of woman we had dressed. I am hoping that when the film is finally put together, there will be a big contrast between her and the other women on screen.'

But, whatever the effect on film, the clothes are authentic to the last detail. Powell, who has a wide knowledge of the history of fashion, brought his own ideas to Zellweger's interpretation. 'I feel, rightly or wrongly – but strongly – that Beatrix's real life was in her imagination,' he says. 'She lived in this extraordinary fantasy

world. She cared nothing for conventions or what people expected her to do. Or how they expected her to look.

'She had been well brought up, so obviously would not go to a meeting with the bank manager or publisher looking a total mess. But, equally, she did not look like the girls and women of her age. She was dressed in a more workmanlike way. So I have gone for a contrast between the way she looked and the way other women appeared in the late 19th and early 20th centuries. This was the time of the full flowering of the *Belle Epoch*. Women tended, on the whole, to be overdressed, over fussy and over-hatted. I tried to make this point.'

Powell also researched family photographs taken by Beatrix's father, Rupert Potter, which covered a period of nearly fifty years. 'A few years ago, a family album

came up for auction,' he says. 'Warne, the publishers, were desperate to have this book but they were outbid by American collectors. Fortunately, the collector who bought it put out a facsimile edition of a hundred copies.'

Powell was able to find a copy from Princeton university and the film-makers bought it. He then based his costumes on the photographs. 'Once you've seen it, then it is the only way to go,' he reasons. 'What I like to do is to give key cast members a wardrobe like normal people. A real person does not wear a different outfit every day. A man of that time, for example, may have had a winter coat, a summer coat, couple of jackets and some shirts, and have put them together in a different way.'

The Making of Miss Potter

Powell hires all the costumes from a company called Cosprop, which has hundreds of racks of old clothes stored in a vast warehouse near Primrose Hill, London. There is also a team of tailors, who make new clothes to original eighteenth and nineteenth century designs. Costume supervisor Rosemary Burrows, who has worked with Powell on several films, picked carefully among the racks and negotiated a budget. The vast store of genuine old shoes is also used. According to actor Bill Paterson (Rupert Potter) it was slipping his feet into a pair of old leather shoes, *circa* 1900, which finally gave him the feel of his time, place and character.

'Every actor has a different approach,' says Powell. 'I like to meet all of them before we start working on their clothes. The difference between theatre and film is that in theatre you can turn an actor into something he is not. With distance from the stage, it can be convincing. You cannot do that on screen, because the beady eye of the camera sees untruths.'

Renée Zellweger presented an immediate problem, even before her requested costume switch. 'She is a modern girl, with a modern figure,' says Powell. 'That means she is slim. This is not the figure of a Victorian or Edwardian woman. Women of Beatrix's class ate more in that period. You only have to look at dinner menus at the time. We would have trouble today getting through the meals. But, oddly, despite being bigger women, they had small waists. They were in corsets from the age of five or six, which deformed the bones while they were still soft.

'The women seemed to have magnificent figures, with no collar bones and round shoulders. The only actress I have ever worked with like that was Bette Davis. She had Edwardian shoulders. But Renée is exceptionally slim. The only way we could get around it was to pad her up under her corset. We originally put her in costumes without padding and it was hopeless. She looked completely wrong.'

Zellweger's fairly plain costumes are in complete contrast with those of Barbara Flynn, who plays her mother, Helen.

'Barbara looks great in a corset,' says Powell. 'I pushed for a big wardrobe for her, because I wanted to show the contrast with the simplicity of Beatrix's clothes. So I overdressed Barbara to make her look rich and glamorous. Her clothes and hair are very fashionable.'

Although most of the dresses are new, made to old styles, every actress was wearing one genuine item: split drawers. 'That is why the can-can was really so frisky at the time,' says Powell. 'All the girls had split knickers. They were like Sharon Stone in *Basic Instinct*. The simple reason was that they were practical for going to the loo.

'There were so many layers of clothes in those days, that it would have taken about fifteen minutes to put on the day clothes and about half an hour for the evening, with jewels and stockings. They would all have had help getting dressed. The poorer women would have helped each other with fastening the corsets up the back. Sometimes, women would have had up to twenty layers of clothes from the skin to the outer garment. So, for our own actresses, the split drawers were very important, for obvious reasons.'

The men, on the other hand, are dressed in a simple and straightforward manner. 'The choice for men of the day was terribly limited,' says Powell. 'They had three cuts of coat – a frock coat, a tail coat and a suit jacket. They were always in dark colours or black. Perhaps with grey trousers, if they were going to be dashing, or even a pinstripe.'

ABOVE *Head of hair and make-up Lisa Westcott attends to Ewan McGregor's face*

BELOW *Make-up artist Graham Johnston makes final adjustments to Renée Zellweger's make-up*

Despite Zellweger's late decision over her wardrobe, Powell is an admirer. 'She is totally single-minded and throws herself into the part,' he says. 'And although she is so disciplined and determined, she has a knack of being enchanting. So there is no resentment and you want to do your best for her.'

Hair and make-up

Renée Zellweger's make-up routine for the film faithfully reflected Beatrix Potter's lack of personal vanity. Graham Johnston, who has been in charge of Zellweger's make-up and hair since the Bridget Jones films, says, 'Renée is exceptional, in the sense that she is prepared to put her own beauty regime aside for the character.' For Beatrix Potter, she was requested to look plain and simple. 'Beatrix was no beauty,' says Johnston, 'so it would have been foolish to portray her that way.'

This meant a daily make-up process of no more than twenty minutes. 'She dyed her own hair with a medium-brown coloured mousse,' says Johnston. 'Then I used make-up which was natural to the eye. Renée has great skin – clear and very peachy.'

In general as little make-up as possible was used for the film. Anthony Powell reports, 'Women of Beatrix Potter's class did not wear any make-up at all at the turn of the last century. Make-up was considered only for tarts or cheap women. If they needed a little colour in their cheeks they used to pinch them. Or they bought little strips of paper to add a little rouge. But no make-up at all was considered best.'

Andrew Dunn: Director of Photography

ABOVE *Director of Photography Andrew Dunn with assistant director Guy Heeley*

As the cinematographer – or lighting cameraman, to give it the film-making description – Andrew Dunn was in charge of lighting and setting a scene to perfection. It is his expertise that makes the film look sharp and realistic.

Dunn has delivered on a range of films, including the Oscar-winning period piece *Gosford Park* (2001) and the contemporary *Sweet Home Alabama* (2002) with Reese Witherspoon. He is likeable, low-key and modest. He also prefers doing to talking. 'My job depends so much on the qualities of others around me,' he insists. 'Do I have a director with skills and confidence? Is there a leading man or woman who is a natural to light? In this film, we've got both. Chris Noonan is a straightforward guy who knows what he wants. Renée Zellweger looks good from virtually every angle. So, for me, I have a ready-made team and the job is a pleasure.'

Martin Childs: Production Designer

Tartan wallpaper surrounding the dining room of the Potter household was the first fixture to set the tone of a Christmas dinner party scene. The scene was then built from the walls, inwards: the right kind of long table, late Victorian heavy furniture, the correct candelabra, table placings and crystal glasses.

It is the sort of detail which helped Martin Childs, 52, win an Oscar for his production design on the big-budget *Shakespeare in Love* or get a Bafta nomination for his efforts on *Mrs Brown* with Dame Judi Dench. He is in charge of the look of the film. He has to examine the script, make suggestions for each scene and begin the long process of hiring every bit of furnishing and all the props, which will be used for the movie.

He is highly experienced, with a wide range of films from the historic (*Quills*) to contemporary (*Calendar Girls*). He has also been a supervising art director on films like *The Portrait of a Lady* (with Nicole Kidman), *The Madness of King George* (Nigel Hawthorne) and *Frankenstein* (with Robert De Niro), directed by Kenneth Branagh.

With *Miss Potter*, Childs needed furnishings from the late 1890s and early 1900s. There were also brief scenes from the 1870s and 1880s. 'I wonder, sometimes, if all the detail is noticed by an audience,' he says. 'But I think that if there was anything wrong, it would just not look right. There are also viewers who are highly aware of

TOP Production designer Martin Childs outside the recreated Hill Top Farm

ABOVE & OPPOSITE BOTTOM Detail of the Potter house set

OPPOSITE TOP & CENTRE Antique props waiting to appear on screen

period and would note every fault. So there's only one way to do the job – and that is to go for total authenticity every time, with every detail.'

The wallpaper is a typical example. 'Tartan was very fashionable at the time,' he says. 'I think it all started off with Queen Victoria and her love of Balmoral. She even had tartan carpets there, apparently. When I worked on *Mrs Brown*, ten years ago, we could not afford any of that because the budget of the film was so small.'

Childs works closely with the director, Chris Noonan, and costume designer, Anthony Powell. It is vital, because the background to a scene may clash with the colour of costumes. 'We discuss such things all the time,' he says. 'I wanted the look of the main drawing room to be rather cool and slightly chilly, because I felt that would reflect the tastes of Beatrix's mother, Mrs Helen Potter.

'We wanted to contrast that rather frosty look with Beatrix's taste. Beatrix lives in this very warm, cosy environment upstairs, where she has not changed the wallpaper since she was a child. This is where she feels at home and is able to get her work done on the books.'

The sets were constructed side-by-side on the Isle of Man's Kirkby industrial estate, next to a lorry base for TransAmerica Leasing.

Says Childs, 'Tina Jones, the set decorator, brings me newspapers or magazines for the period and we choose a certain look. She will

look for fabrics for the furniture. So all the furniture we get in for a scene is adapted for our use. We might re-cover chairs or choose drapes to give the right background.'

All the furnishings were hired from one of several companies scattered around west London. Vast warehouses are crammed with furniture from all periods, awaiting hire by the BBC or film companies. 'The interior of the Potter household has probably been furnished by six or seven companies,' says Childs. 'Tina has been around them, in person, to pick every item.

'They are then shipped by the prop master (Allen Polley) to whichever location we need them. On *Miss Potter*, we were setting up the household interiors on the Isle of Man. We needed drivers to pack up all the furnishings, get to Liverpool, put the trucks on the ferry and drive to our location.

'There is always a certain amount of "hurry up", whatever film you are on. There is never too much time or money. When you find out what your budget is, along with the prep time, you never think, "Oh, that is more than I need." Every time I design sets, it always seems to cost about thirty per cent more than I have at my disposal.

The Making of Miss Potter

'So, before we start the hiring and building process, we do little negotiations with the producers to settle on a sum. I occasionally had a slap on the wrist from the art director (Grant Armstrong), who held the purse strings.'

Childs' first action was to draw up plans, at a quarter inch to the foot, so he could work out all interior planning for where furniture would be placed. He had to also work out camera angles with the director. The Christmas dining room scene, for example, allows a camera to scan the whole length of the table, with close-ups on each character.

The walls of the sets were partly assembled in London's Elstree studios from the drawings by Childs, under the watchful eye of their construction manager. They were then shipped out in flat-pack form to the Isle of Man. All the mouldings, cornice work and hand rails were added on site.

Construction in the former cowshed and industrial site began about six weeks before the furniture arrived. 'The great thing about this period of history, with its wealthy families, is that the people look wonderful in their costumes,' says Childs. 'My job is to set them off in the right mood. By the time the actors arrive, everything is in its place and worked out.'

ABOVE & BELOW *The Potters' dining room. A 30-foot crane for the camera stretches over the dinner table*

OPPOSITE TOP
Beatrix's study

OPPOSITE BOTTOM
Property master Allen Polley

Chapter Eight

PLAYING IT FOR REAL

Emily Watson plays Millie Warne

Emily Watson twice turned down her role as Millie Warne, sister of the tragic Norman, who became Beatrix's best friend. She had given birth to her first baby, Juliet, born in November 2005, and felt that it was too early to return in front of the film cameras. 'I was still breast feeding, so I just thought, "Oh, shut up and go away,"' she says.

But Watson, 39, who married in 1995, was persuaded to change her mind by director Chris Noonan. 'It was bit by bit,' she says. 'I loved *Babe*, the film which Chris made, and thought it would be great to work with a person like him. Then, I found myself asking how many days it would be. When they said it would take ten days, I thought it might be rather nice, because it would kick-start getting my working life back on track again.'

Watson, who has won two Oscar nominations for best actress (*Breaking the Waves*, her movie debut, in 1996 and *Hilary and Jackie*, 1998), was also lured by the fact that the part is well written. 'Supporting roles usually mean that you do a few scenes as a wife or girlfriend,' she says. 'But this one was interesting and liberating.'

The fact that Millie was genuinely close to Beatrix – they continued to correspond for the rest of their lives, after Norman's death – added an interesting twist. 'It is another dimension to the film,' says Watson. 'It is not just a sad love story, but a story about women and what it means to be a spinster. They were both single women in their late thirties who had found a common bond. And to be an artist and single in those days must have been tough.

'There was also no acceptance at the time of a woman moving out of the family home and living alone. It might only be a century ago, but it was a different world.

'Those times were tough, at whatever level of society you lived. Women like Millie and Beatrix were frustrated by the society they lived in and its limitations.'

Women did not have the vote and, once they married, their husband owned them. They took over their possessions and controlled their lives, perfectly legally. The First World War changed everything, once women proved they could do men's jobs.'

To get Watson to play the role of Millie was something of a coup. After establishing a reputation as a leading theatre actress, with the Royal Shakespeare Company, she has been hired for a succession of movie leads. Her screen performances have always been well reviewed, even when the film itself has fallen short of box office expectations. She starred in *The Mill on the Floss* (1997), *The Boxer* (also 1997), *Angela's Ashes* (1999), *Punch-Drunk Love* (2002) and *Red Dragon* (also 2002).

But Watson has a distinctive style. She does not deliver the glamour roles, but plays women with flaws, both physical and emotional, with whom an audience can empathise. 'The first thing I said to Chris Noonan, when I finally agreed to play Millie, was that I wanted to play her plump,' she says. 'And as she was not a beautiful woman who was particularly interested in men, it did not really matter.'

Watson has a refreshing approach to body image, compared to weight-obsessed Hollywood. 'I have not lost weight quickly after giving birth,' she says. 'I think that is dangerous. As soon as I got the job, I did an hour and a half of Pilates every day. But there was no way I was going down the gym. Your body is full of hormones and you shouldn't be made to exercise.'

The role also reintroduced Watson to the dreaded corsets, *circa* 1905. 'They are unbearable to wear – so uncomfortable,' she says. 'It is like having a stiff piece of cardboard around your middle. It affects everything – the way you move, the way you breathe and the way you sit. It must have been desperately unhealthy for the women of those days. No wonder so many of them looked so pained in the old photographs.

'I did a film in corsets before I got pregnant (*The Proposition*) and we were working in the searing heat of a little town in Queensland, Australia. It was agony.'

Her research into life one hundred years ago has given Watson a clear view of how things have changed. 'Those times were tough, at whatever level of society you lived,' she asserts. 'Women like Millie and Beatrix were frustrated by the society they lived in and its limitations. But, in Australia, we worked in a little town where the cemetery was full of women in their early twenties who died in childbirth. These were not great times.'

Watson is also typically frank and forthright about how motherhood has changed her own life. 'Towards the end of my pregnancy, I was really exhausted and enormous,' she says. 'As for having a baby in the house, it

The Making of Miss Potter

was mind-boggling. I thought, "How am I ever, ever, ever going to be able to act in anything, ever again?" It would be six o'clock in the evening and I was still in my pyjamas. But times go by, our daughter is fantastic and we are having a lovely time.'

Watson's wide experience – she's packed twenty-five major film performances into ten years – has given her a routine which works for her. 'I find the most useful preparation for a part is done in my own home,' she says. 'I prepare well ahead of time. I work out the logic of it – like why Millie thinks and feels as she does. And if the film is well written, like *Miss Potter*, it is easier to make it work.

'So actual rehearsals with the rest of the cast, for me, are often an embarrassment. I hate the sound of my own voice and feel that everyone is thinking, "Oh, God, she's not going to do it like that, is she?" I don't want to nail something before it goes on camera, because I fear I might not get it back again.'

But Emily Watson seemed to time her key moments particularly well in *Miss Potter*. And she has some sharp observations on Beatrix herself. 'I think, on reflection, that her books are not all cute,' she says. 'They do have a darkness to them, despite being written for children. When you look at her life, the people she mixed with and the personal tragedy, it perhaps goes some way to explain things.'

ABOVE *Millie (Emily Watson) and Beatrix (Renée Zellweger) enjoy a spirited discussion about the advantages of spinsterhood*

BELOW *Bill Paterson as Rupert Potter*

OPPOSITE *Mr Potter (Bill Paterson) in his younger days indulging in his favourite hobby, photography*

Bill Paterson plays Rupert Potter

Bill Paterson was in for an early surprise when he agreed to take on the role of Beatrix's father, Rupert. His days would start with two and a half hours of make-up. The real Mr Potter had insisted on growing a huge pair of whiskers, known in the 1860s as dundrearies, which he never shaved off for the remainder of his

life. The whiskers were worn by a London stage actor, E. H. Sothern, now long forgotten. Edward Sothern, born in Liverpool in 1829, had moved to America in 1851 where he successfully played the lead, Lord Dundreary, in 1,100 performances of the play *Our American Cousin*, by Tom Taylor. He moved with the play to London, where it was staged at the Haymarket Theatre. The play became a hit, Sothern was a sensation and, in particular, so were his giant sideburns. They became fashionable for around twenty years.

'In Rupert Potter's case, he never moved on from that fashion,' says Paterson. 'He clearly didn't ever shave again and he lived to 82. The big chops became grey with age – and that was about it.' Paterson, 61, has to play Rupert Potter during his sixties for much of the film. But there are flashbacks to the 1870s and 80s, when the whiskers had to be darker and the hair less bald.

'I never usually do long make-up days, so it is all a bit strange for me,' he says. 'I must have become a bit lazy over the years, playing doctors, teachers or police officers. I usually just have to come in and perform.'

Paterson, a Scot who has built a highly successful career delivering consistently well, mostly on stage or on television, did not think he would be in the running to play Mr Potter. 'It very much hangs on distinction with a role like this,' he says. 'I can play all sorts, but they generally tend to be Scottish people. But the director Chris Noonan thought I was the man for the job – and with the help of the dialect coach, Barbara Berkery, I have an English accent.'

He is surprised at Mr Potter's lifestyle, a century ago. 'He seems to have spent most of his time either at the Reform Club or following his hobby of photography, which was in its infancy in the 1860s. He had inherited a fortune, kept servants and could devote himself to other interests.'

Despite reports that Beatrix was closer to her father than her mother, Paterson is uncertain how the relationship would appear today.

'Beatrix seemed to spend a lot of her childhood in the third floor nursery of her home,' he says. 'So I would judge that her father had a slightly distant, odd relationship with her. But, compared to her mother and others in her life, perhaps it seemed warm to her.'

ABOVE *Mr Potter (Bill Paterson) at the family breakfast table*

BELOW *Paterson presents a cake on set to celebrate Ewan McGregor's birthday*

Paterson, who has a 21-year-old son and 16-year-old daughter, says, 'I think, overall, we have a far closer and more loving relationship with our children. It is far less formal. That was just the way it was in those days with people who had money.'

But he enjoyed playing the role. 'It got me into the Reform Club, to have another look, and I don't think the place has changed much,' he says. 'Mr Potter would

recognise it straight away, apart from the odd computer screen downstairs for security. It also has a fantastic library, a menu which looked a bit school dinner-ish and a pleasing atmosphere. Mr Potter, who worked hard at his leisure, must have really felt at home.'

Why would Norman Warne have been considered an unsuitable husband? 'You have to get into the mindset of high Victorian society,' he says. 'Publishing was thought of as "trade". Both Mr and Mrs Potter came from industrial families in the north of England and the right kind of match in marriage would have been to someone else from industry, living their kind of life.'

The Making of Miss Potter

And why could Beatrix not have enjoyed more support from her parents? 'It is one of the great questions of the film and something I've pondered over,' he says. 'It is one of the great enigmas, why they did not approve of her marrying into a respectable family, like the Warnes. I suppose you need to be sitting there at the time, living in fear that your family fortune might disappear if it fell in to the wrong hands.'

ABOVE Mrs Potter (Barbara Flynn) takes the Lakeland air with her children, Beatrix (Lucy Boynton) and Bertram (Oliver Jenkins)

BELOW Mr and Mrs Potter (Bill Paterson and Barbara Flynn) relax on holiday in the Lake District

Barbara Flynn plays Mrs Helen Potter

Barbara Flynn defends the lingering image of Helen Potter as a snob and social climber. 'She wanted the best for her family – and her daughter,' she says. 'I do not believe in playing her as a dreadful woman. She is protective and complicated.'

Helen Potter also socialised regularly, even though it was with a narrow social class. There were house parties and dinners which were like virtual feasts. On May 7th, 1875, when Beatrix was nine, the menu for a dinner party at the Potters' home at 2 Bolton Gardens, South Kensington was as follows: 'spring soup, salmon, sweetbreads, lobster cutlets, spring chickens, ham, roast lamb, ducklings and peas, mousseline pudding, jelly, cherry ice and brown bread rice'.

Playing It For Real 85

Flynn, 58, certainly adds some warmth to someone who sounds, from reputation, chilly and calculating. 'I am not looking for sympathy for Helen,' she says. 'But I understand her. She always looks terribly bad-tempered in all the old photographs. The pictures were taken by her husband. I know my father took plenty of photographs of my mother and she looked bad-tempered in those, too. But she wasn't in real life.'

Like other key cast members, Flynn has carefully researched her role. 'There is extra responsibility when playing a woman who really lived,' she reasons. 'Helen said that she was very much like her own mother, with whom she got on very well. They enjoyed sewing together and discussed things like hats and dresses. She was quite a tasteful woman and I am sure when she had Beatrix she hoped a similar sort of relationship would develop to the one she enjoyed with her own mother.'

But it was not to be. 'Life has a way of presenting huge, thumping ironies and Beatrix was nothing like her mother expected or wanted,' says Flynn. 'Helen Potter felt so thwarted by Beatrix not wanting to marry well. Instead, her child turned into this extraordinary and talented human being who would have been so much more suited to living in the north rather than being stuck in smart Bolton Gardens in London.'

ABOVE *Mr Potter (Bill Paterson) and Mrs Potter (Barbara Flynn) confront their tomboy daughter Beatrix (Lucy Boynton), covered from head to toe in mud*

The film starts at a point when Beatrix Potter is enjoying her early triumph with the publication of *The Tale of Peter Rabbit*. 'For Helen, this is when she is at her most confused about her daughter,' says Flynn. 'She cannot control her; she's in her thirties and lives in her own world in her top bedroom. This is a world in which Helen does not belong.'

Flynn, from Hastings, East Sussex, who has been married since 1982 and has a son, launched her television career in 1970 in *A Family at War*. She has since amassed high profile roles in forty-seven TV series or dramas, but has a limited number of movie appearances.

'I can only think they chose me in this because I love corsets,' she jokes. 'Even when I was as slim as glamorous Renée Zellweger, I loved corsets. I am now blessed with the sort of shape that works with them. If you are straight up and down, it's not so easy. I love dressing up – that's one of the reasons I became an actress in the first place.'

She is also taking a risk for an actress – actually ageing up, with make-up and hair alterations. Actresses are usually obsessed with losing years from their real age, not gaining them.

'It takes hours to make me look this old,' she laughs. 'But I enjoy immersing myself in the Potters' world.'

Chapter Nine

LOCATION, LOCATION, LOCATION

>—⊶——◦——⊷—<

'There is never enough time. That is the only thing you can rely on with films.'

*I*t is hard to recall when a Hollywood-based star last looked so unglamorous in a film. But Renée Zellweger is wearing the dingiest brown floor-length skirt, with a large woollen shawl, as she walks along a rutted lane in the heart of the Lake District.

She is playing Beatrix Potter in late summer of 1905, still in mourning after the sudden death of her fiancé. Miss Potter eventually bought her first farm, Hill Top in Sawrey, in November 1905, to begin a new stage of her life three hundred miles north of the luxurious London home she still shared with her parents.

The location of Hill Top, now owned by the National Trust as are all fifteen farms in the Lake District which Miss Potter gifted on her death, is unsuitable for a film set. So the location manager, Martin Joy, and Lake District location manager Beverley Lamb, have chosen instead another of her original farms, Yew Tree.

Production designer Martin Childs and his team have started work days before Zellweger and the film crew arrive. The result is a complete transformation. The front of the farmhouse of Lakeland slate is repainted from its usual white to a greeny-grey mixture. The garden is planted with summer flowers. Even a dry stone wall has been constructed in a week, to match the one at Hill Top around the start of the century. There are also rows of fake beans and a cluster of fake roses. But they look like the real thing in the morning sunshine which has emerged from the sweeping hills of Holme Fell and Yewdale Fell.

A pig pen constructed opposite the farm, though, does not meet with director Chris Noonan's approval. 'Having worked with pigs,' he tell Childs, 'I know they always need a covered area on one side of the pen. It would not be realistic to have it open.' Work begins immediately.

In the lane, where Zellweger is waiting to film, an exact replica of an old advertising bill has been hammered in to a post. It reads: 'Hill Top. For Sale. Farm and dwelling house with a large and productive garden and appurtenances belonging thereto, presently without occupation. Messrs W. Heelis & Co. Solicitors.'

Zellweger's take is simple. She picks up a stone, knocks the sign off the gate and, with a smile, takes it with her. It announces, wordlessly, that Beatrix Potter is ready for a new life.

But, in counterpoint to the re-creation of this scene of fresh beginnings a century ago, there is a sobering note in the local newspaper. The nearby Sedbergh Auction Mart, which has been held since the 13th century, is to close. Hill farming is in desperate straits and even Jon and Caroline Watson, today's tenant farmers of the 600-acre Yew Tree Farm, have been badly hit. They have 300 sheep and 14 cows on the farm. Jon Watson reports, 'I sold my first sheep at the age of 14 for £40. I am still getting exactly the same price today – and I am 43. Farming really is dying.'

In the farm building, there are chairs and sideboards which were chosen by Beatrix Potter when she owned the place. 'She would have been sad at the state of things now,' says Watson. 'But it is great to stand here and see what it must have been like at the start of the 20th century. The transformation is so good that we hardly recognise the place – and we live here.'

This is a joy to hear for the location managers and production designers who have been able to turn the clock back.

The Yew Tree Farm transformation is one of many in the film. A full list of the locations is included on page 94.

The Making of Miss Potter

Animation

Simon Stanley-Clamp, who worked on all the Harry Potter films, was in charge of bringing animals like Peter Rabbit and Jemima Puddle-duck to life. The animation is spread through a few key sequences during the film, but runs to a total of 90 seconds. 'This is pure, old-fashioned animation,' he says. 'We wanted to stick close to the true style of Potter, with the hand-drawn frames.'

ABOVE AND BELOW
Visual effects supervisor Simon Stanley-Clamp works out a special effects shot with Renée Zellweger for the scene where Beatrix paints furiously in an agony of grief after Norman's death

RIGHT *Sketches for the animated sequence of moving drawings which express the turmoil in her mind*

While the filming was going on in the Isle of Man and the Lake District there were a team of animation artists working in London. They were delivering twelve separate drawings, slightly altered to show movement, for each second of film. 'We decided to avoid computers,' says Stanley-Clamp. 'It is a series of pencil drawings or water colours.'

Film Editing

Film editor Robin Sales was working against the clock to deliver a rough cut of *Miss Potter* just one week after filming was completed. It meant that he spent long hours in the editing suite, shaping and editing the results of Chris Noonan's succession of daily takes on different scenes. The result is that more than a thousand minutes of film is eventually cut to around a hundred minutes.

The film was sent at 4 p.m. each day by courier to London to night-time laboratories at Technicolor. Technicians would develop the film overnight and the tapes would be sent back, again by courier, the following morning to Sales' editing suite. 'I look at them, make various notes and then put everything together during the afternoon,' says Sales. 'What I am doing is assembling a vast jigsaw.'

So how does he know which take to use? 'There are notes from the script supervisor, like "Chris preferred take five." But you are looking all the time and making your own mental notes all the time. A scene might be a bit of take three, linked to take six, for example. It all depends on the shot.'

This is the beginning of such a long post-production process that Sales' job does not end until just before release. Since the first preview is planned for late July and the film is not completed until early May, there is a strict deadline. The preview audience will not be hearing the film's music – the *Shakespeare in Love* score is being used instead – because the music is still being written by Australian composer Nigel Westlake.

What is called the 'final film lock' is planned for September. After that, the sound and final music is added, with extra dialogue and voices. 'There is,' smiles Sales, 'never enough time. That is the only thing you can rely on with films.'

ABOVE *Editor Robin Sales*

LEFT *Portable darkroom for loading camera film*

BELOW *Editor Robin Sales in discussion with director Chris Noonan*

APPENDIX

Locations in Miss Potter

Interior of printers': Type Museum, 100 Hackford Road, London SW9.

Interior of art gallery: Osterley House, Jersey Road, Brentford, Middlesex.

Exterior, in Hyde Park – carriage driving: Osterley House, Jersey Road, Brentford, Middlesex.

Interior of Warne house: 19 The Butts, Brentford, Middlesex.

Exterior of Warne house: 15 The Butts, Brentford, Middlesex.

Exterior of Warne house gardens: 14 Liverpool Road, Kingston-on-Thames.

Interior and exterior of Potter house: 4 St Peter's Square, London W6.

Interior and exterior of book shop: Nigel Williams Rare Books, 25 Cecil Court, London WC2.

Euston railway station, both interior and exterior: The Bluebell Line, Horsted Keynes, East Sussex.

Interior and exterior of Warne's office: Lincolns Inn, 11a New Square, London WC2 and Wildy's bookshop, 4 New Square.

Interior and exterior of the Reform Club: The Reform Club, 104 Pall Mall, London SW1.

Exterior Hill Top Farm, Lake District: Yew Tree Farm.

Lake District, walking trail: Loughrigg Terrace, Grasmere.

Potter house, drawing room, hallway, living room and conservatory: Lheakrow Farm, Foxdale, Isle of Man.

Interior Potter house, landing, Beatrix's room, nursery, bedroom: Unit 6, Kirby Farm, Isle of Man.

Interior Hill Top Farm, kitchen, parlour, living room and interior of Warne offices: Unit 6, Kirby Farm, Isle of Man.

Interior train compartment in 1877 and 1902: Unit 6, Kirby Farm, Isle of Man.

MISS POTTER
Cast List

Beatrix Potter	RENÉE ZELLWEGER
Norman Warne	EWAN McGREGOR
Millie Warne	EMILY WATSON
Mrs Potter	BARBARA FLYNN
Rupert Potter	BILL PATERSON
Miss Wiggin	MATYELOK GIBBS
William Heelis	LLOYD OWEN
Harold Warne	ANTON LESSER
Fruing Warne	DAVID BAMBER
Fiona	PATRICIA KERRIGAN
Hilda	JUDITH BARKER
Saunders	CHRISTOPHER MIDDLETON
Young Beatrix	LUCY BOYNTON
Young Bertram	OLIVER JENKINS
Ashton Clifford	RICHARD MULHOLLAND
Lady Clifford	SARAH CROWDEN
Lady Stokely	BRIDGET McCONNEL
Lady Sybil	LYNN FARLEIGH
Mr Copperthwaite	GEOFFREY BEEVERS
Mrs Haddon-Bell	CLARE CLIFFORD
Mrs Warne	PHYLLIDA LAW
Sir Nigel	JOHN WOODVINE
Mr Cannon	MARC FINN
Lady Armitage	JANE HOW
Young Heelis	JUSTIN McDONALD
Jane	JENNIFER CASTLE
Well-dressed Woman	AVRIL CLARK
Lionel Stokely	JOSEPH GRIEVES
Harry Haddon-Bell	ANDY McSORLEY
Auctioneer	DOMINIC KEMP
George Brown	NICHOLAS HUTCHINSON
Auction Bidder	BARRY McCORMICK
Lands Trust Member	MIKE BURNSIDE

The Author: Garth Pearce

Garth Pearce, a regular writer for the *Sunday Times*, has reported from more than five hundred film sets in thirty-five countries. He is a former Fleet Street show-business editor who has interviewed almost every major star. He works for leading publications such as the *Scotsman*, the *Australian* and the *New York Times* syndicate. *The Making of Miss Potter* is his eighth book.

The Photographer: Alex Bailey

Alex Bailey specializes in film and television photography. His work is often seen in books, magazines, newspapers and as movie posters, and has received much acclaim both in the UK and internationally.